# 85 classic recipes
# Indian

# 85 classic recipes
# Indian

easy-to-make, authentic and delicious dishes, shown
step by step in more than 350 sizzling photographs

Rafi Fernandez

**southwater**

This edition is published by Southwater, an imprint of Anness Publishing Ltd, Hermes House, 88–89 Blackfriars Road, London SE1 8HA; tel. 020 7401 2077; fax 020 7633 9499; www.southwaterbooks.com; www.annesspublishing.com

If you like the images in this book and would like to investigate using them for publishing, promotions or advertising, please visit our website www.practicalpictures.com for more information.

UK agent: The Manning Partnership Ltd; tel. 01225 478444; fax 01225 478440; sales@manning-partnership.co.uk
UK distributor: Grantham Book Services Ltd; tel. 01476 541080; fax 01476 541061; orders@gbs.tbs-ltd.co.uk
North American agent/distributor: National Book Network; tel. 301 459 3366; fax 301 429 5746; www.nbnbooks.com
Australian agent/distributor: Pan Macmillan Australia; tel. 1300 135 113; fax 1300 135 103; customer.service@macmillan.com.au
New Zealand agent/distributor: David Bateman Ltd; tel. (09) 415 7664; fax (09) 415 8892

Publisher: Joanna Lorenz
Project Editors: Lindsay Porter, Linda Doeser
Photography: Edward Allwright
Design: David Rowley Design, Siân Keogh
Styling: Maria Kelly
Production Controller: Don Campaniello

Recipes on pages 80, 81 and 92 by Stephen Wheeler. Recipes on pages 87 and 88 by Deh-Ta Hsiung.

ETHICAL TRADING POLICY
Because of our ongoing ecological investment programme, you, as our customer, can have the pleasure and reassurance of knowing that a tree is being cultivated on your behalf to naturally replace the materials used to make the book you are holding. For further information about this scheme, go to www.annesspublishing.com/trees

Previously published as *Great Indian Dishes*

NOTES
Bracketed terms are intended for American readers.
For all recipes, quantities are given in both metric and imperial measures and, where appropriate, in standard cups and spoons.
Follow one set of measures, but not a mixture, because they are not interchangeable.
Standard spoon and cup measures are level. 1 tsp = 5ml, 1 tbsp = 15ml, 1 cup = 250ml/8fl oz.
Australian standard tablespoons are 20ml. Australian readers should use 3 tsp in place of 1 tbsp for measuring small quantities.
American pints are 16fl oz/2 cups. American readers should use 20fl oz/2.5 cups in place of 1 pint when measuring liquids.
Electric oven temperatures in this book are for conventional ovens. When using a fan oven, the temperature will probably need to be reduced by about 10–20°C/20–40°F. Since ovens vary, you should check with your manufacturer's instruction book for guidance.
The nutritional analysis given for each recipe is calculated per portion (i.e. serving or item), unless otherwise stated. If the recipe gives a range, such as Serves 4–6, then the nutritional analysis will be for the smaller portion size, i.e. 6 servings. Measurements for sodium do not include salt added to taste. Medium (US large) eggs are used unless otherwise stated.

Front cover shows Hot and Sour Meat and Lentil Curry – for recipe see page 56

# CONTENTS

Introduction  6

Starters and Snacks  10

Rice and Bread  18

Meat Dishes  28

Poultry and Egg Dishes  38

Seafood Dishes  48

Pulses and Lentils  56

Vegetable Dishes  66

Chutneys, Pickles and Salads  76

Desserts and Drinks  84

Stockists and Suppliers  93

Index  94

# INTRODUCTION

The vast sub-continent of India offers a range of culinary delights as rich and diverse as its people and history. Each region has its own unique cooking style. Cream, yoghurt, ghee and nuts feature in dishes from the north, while the south favours chillies, coconut and coconut oil. Fish and mustard oil predominate in the east, while the west has incorporated the greatest number of foreign ingredients. The story of Indian cusine is also one of religion. The south, for example, is predominantly Hindu and consequently vegetarian, with pulses fulfilling an important nutritional role. While meat is eaten in the Muslim north, this does not, of course, include pork. One element unites these diverse styles – the use of herbs and spices to create the flavours and aromas distinctive of Indian cuisine.

❧

This book begins with a useful glossary of specialist equipment and some of the more unfamiliar spices and ingredients. The recipes that follow are divided into nine chapters: Starters and Snacks, Rice and Bread, Meat Dishes, Poultry and Egg Dishes, Seafood Dishes, Pulses and Lentils, Vegetable Dishes, Chutneys, Pickles and Salads, and Desserts and Drinks. All the recipes are superbly illustrated in colour with easy-to-follow step-by-step instructions. Hints and tips offer helpful suggestions and variations of the recipes.

❧

All the recipes have been tested with the Western kitchen in mind, so whether your tastes lie with a spicy chicken curry or aromatic steamed fish, Indian ice cream or hot lime pickle, success is virtually guaranteed.

# THE PRINCIPLES OF INDIAN COOKING

The Indian diet is the product of many influences – economic, religious and environmental – but Indian meals will combine nutrition with a harmonious blend of textures and flavours. For this reason, care must be taken to provide the correct accompaniment to any dish. Cooling elements such as raithas and salads should be served with hot curries, with pickles and chutneys providing the perfect foil to heavily spiced dishes. There is no myth to Indian cooking. Each of the dishes in this book can be easily prepared in the Western kitchen, and the majority of ingredients are readily available in supermarkets.

## EQUIPMENT AND UTENSILS

**Chappati griddle (tava)** (1) These are made from heavy wrought iron and allow chappatis and other breads to be cooked without burning.

**Chappati rolling board (roti takta)** (2) This board consists of a round wooden surface on stubby legs and helps in shaping different sizes of breads. The extra height helps disperse excess dry flour.

**Chappati rolling pin (velan)** (3) These are thinner in shape than Western pins and come in a variety of sizes. Use whichever best suits your hand.

**Chappati spoon (roti chamcha)** (4) The square-shaped flat head assists in roasting breads on the hot griddle.

**Colander (channi)** (5) Use a sturdy, stainless steel colander as it will not discolour.

**Food processor** (6) This is an essential piece of equipment. Small quantities of ingredients can be ground using a pestle and mortar or a coffee grinder.

**Heat diffuser** (7) Many curries are simmered gently over a low heat, and a heat diffuser helps prevent burning on the base.

**Indian frying pan (karai)** (8) A karai is similar to a wok but is more rounded in shape and made of heavier metal.

**Knives (churrie)** (9) Keep knives very sharp. It will be easier to chop ingredients and will ensure neat edges.

**Oblong grinding stone and pin (sil padi)** (10) This is a traditional Indian 'food processor'. The ingredients are placed on a stone made of heavy slate marked with notches. The rolling pin is used to pulverize the ingredients against the stone.

**Rice spoon (chawal ke chamchi)** (11) This helps prevent the rice grains from being damaged while serving.

**Sizzler (garam thali)** (12) This enables food to be served at the table still cooking.

**Slotted spoon (channi chamchi)** (13) This enables items to be removed safely from deep hot oil or other liquids.

**Stainless steel pestle and mortar (hamam dasta)** (14) This is ideal for grinding small amounts of wet ingredients such as ginger and garlic. The steel is everlasting and will not retain the strong flavours of the spices.

**Stone pestle and mortar (pathar hamam dasta)** (15) This is suitable for mixing small amounts of ingredients, both wet and dry.

## SPICES

**Aniseed** (1) This has a delicate liquorice flavour and sweet seeds. It is a good aid to digestion.

**Bay leaves** (2) Bay leaves feature in a lot of dishes from the north of India. They are also used in aromatic rice.

**Black cardamom** (3) These large black pods are used whole. They have a menthol aroma and are mainly used in cooking from the north of India.

**Black cumin** (4) These aromatic seeds are mainly used whole sprinkled on breads and in rice dishes. Do not substitute with ordinary cumin seeds.

**Chilli powder** (5) Many brands are now available and each vary in spiciness. Add small quantities at a time and adjust accordingly.

**Cinnamon bark** (6) This is also available in quill form. It can be removed from the dish before serving.

**Cloves** (7) Cloves are used in both savoury and sweet dishes.

**Coriander powder** (8) Coriander powder not only adds flavour but is also used to thicken curries.

**Coriander seeds** (9) Coriander seeds are very rarely used whole. Dry-roast the seeds before grinding. Coriander is essential to a good curry.

**Cumin powder** (10) Highly aromatic cumin powder is one of the essential ingredients in curries.

**Cumin seeds** (11) Whole cumin seeds are mainly used in vegetarian dishes. Dry-roast the seeds before grinding.

**Fennel seeds** (12) The seeds of the fennel are aromatic and sweet. They may be used whole or in powdered form. They are also dry-roasted, cooled and served after meals to aid digestion and freshen the mouth.

**Fenugreek powder** (13) This slightly bitter-tasting ingredient must be used sparingly.

**Fenugreek seeds** (14) These are used whole in vegetarian dishes. When planted the seed produces a spinach.

**Five-spice powder** (15) This is a combination of star anise, fennel, cinnamon, clove and Sichuan pepper.

**Garam masala** (16) This combination of spices provides heat to the body and enhances curries. Several combinations are available.

**Green cardamom** (17) Green cardamom is sweet and aromatic in flavour and is used in both savoury and sweet dishes.

**Mustard seeds** (18) Mustard seeds are odourless but become very pungent when pounded or moistened. When planted they produce mustard spinach.

**Nigella** (19) Nigella is an aromatic spice with a sharp and tingling taste. It is mainly used in vegetarian dishes.

**Onion seeds** (20) These black teardrop-shaped seeds have an earthy aroma. They are sprinkled on breads and used in vegetarian dishes.

**Peppercorns** (21) Peppercorns were introduced to India by the Portuguese and are now an indispensable ingredient in much Indian cooking.

**Red chillies** (22) Red chillies were introduced to India by the Portuguese. The larger the chilli the less hot it is. Remove the seeds for a milder chilli taste.

**Round red chillies** (23) These are hot, with a pimento flavour and are delicious in pickles.

**Saffron** (24) Saffron is the world's most expensive spice, produced from the stigma of a particular variety of crocus. Over 100,000 crocus blossoms picked by hand are needed to produce 450g (1lb) of saffron.

**Star anise** (25) Star anise is a star-shaped, liquorice-flavoured pod.

**Turmeric** (26) Turmeric is yellow in colour with an earthy but pungent taste. It should be used with caution.

# INGREDIENTS

**Almond flakes** (1) Almond flakes are extremely rich in vitamin B1. They are prohibitively expensive in India.

**Apricots** (2) Apricots are mainly used for festive occasions and celebrations. Stewed apricots are served with custard as a favourite dessert.

**Asafoetida** (3) This is a resin with an acrid and bitter taste and a strong odour. Store in a jar with a strong air-tight seal to prevent the smell dispersing into other ingredients.

**Aubergine (egg plant)** (4) Immerse aubergines (egg plant) in water immediately after cutting to prevent discoloration.

**Basmati rice** (5) Basmati rice is the staple grain of India. Many brands are now available in the West.

**Bengal gram** (6) Bengal gram is used whole in lentil curries. The flour (besan) is used to prepare bhajias and may be used to flavour and thicken certain curries.

**Black-eyed beans** (7) These are oval-shaped beige beans with a distinctive dark 'eye'. They are very popular in the north of India.

**Black gram** (8) Black gram may be used whole or split. The flour is used to make papadums.

**Bottle gourd** (9) The fruit of the bottle gourd is whitish-green. Remove peel and pith before using.

**Chick peas (garbanzo beans)** (10) These are beige heart-shaped peas, sold dry or cooked soaked in brine. Pre-cooked, soaked chick peas (garbanzo beans) save a lot of preparation time.

**Coriander leaves** (11) Coriander is India's most popular herb, and is well-loved for its refreshing and unique taste and aroma.

**Curry leaves** (12) Curry leaves are most popular in the south of India. The leaves freeze well without any special preparation.

**Gentleman's toes (tindla)** (13) These tender fruits look like mini cucumbers when cut. If over-ripe they will be red inside.

**Ginger** (14) Fresh ginger is essential to Indian cuisine and is used in a wide variety of sweet and savoury dishes.

**Green chillies** (15) Green chillies are not indigenous to India but have become indispensable to Indian cuisine. They are very rich in vitamins A and C.

**Gypsy beans** (16) These have a slightly bitter taste but are delicious when cooked. Top and tail like any other bean before using.

**Indian cheese (paneer)** (17) Paneer is extremely popular in the north of India and is used in many vegetarian dishes for added nutrition. Long-life vacuum-packed paneer is available from Indian supermarkets and many health food shops.

**Lemon** (18) Lemons and limes are used to sour curries and make pickles and chutneys.

**Mace** (19) Mace is the dried covering of the nutmeg. It has a slightly bitter taste.

**Mango (ripe)** (20) Several varieties of mango are available but the best, 'alfonso', can only be found between May and July.

**Mango (green)** (21) Green mangoes are mainly used to make pickles and chutneys. They are sometimes added to south Indian curries.

**Melon** (22) Melon is often served in India for its cooling qualities.

**Mint** (23) Indian mint has a stronger aroma than the varieties available in the West.

**Nutmeg** (24) This aromatic and sweet spice is essential to many Indian dishes.

**Okra** (25) Okra is a very popular vegetable in India. It must be prepared and cooked with care to prevent the sticky insides from spreading among other ingredients in a dish.

**Oranges** (26) Oranges are refreshing served in wedges after a meal.

**Pistachios** (27) Pistachios are not indigenous to India and are therefore an expensive ingredient.

**Purple beans** (28) These beans have a broad, greenish purple pod with dark purple seeds. Top and tail before using.

**Red chillies** (29) Fresh red chillies vary in strength. The hottest are the smallest, known as 'bird's eyes'.

**Red gram** (30) Red gram is available dry or lightly oiled.

**Red onion** (31) Red onions are in fact a deep purple colour. They are more pungent than ordinary onions.

**Santra** (32) Santra is very refreshing after a curry meal. Serve wedges sprinkled with salt and pepper.

**Spinach** (33) India has over 15 varieties of spinach and it features in many vegetarian dishes.

**Tamarind** (34) Tamarind is a sour crescent-shaped fruit.

**Tomato** (35) The tomato is another ingredient introduced to India by the Portuguese, which now features in many dishes.

**Vermicelli** (36) These hair-like strands are made from wheat and are used in savoury and sweet dishes. Indian is much finer than Italian vermicelli.

**Walnuts** (37) Walnuts are used in sweetmeats, salads and raitha.

# ONION FRITTERS

### *Bhajias*

Bhajias are a classic snack of India. The same batter may be used with a variety of vegetables.

| MAKES 20–25 | 1 tsp turmeric powder | 2 large onions, finely sliced |
|---|---|---|
| | 1 tsp baking powder | 2 green chillies, finely chopped |
| **Ingredients** | ¼ tsp asafoetida | 50g/2oz coriander leaves, chopped |
| 225g/8oz gram flour (besan), or channa atta | salt, to taste | cold water, to mix |
| ½ tsp chilli powder | ½ tsp each, nigella, fennel, cumin and onion seeds, coarsely crushed | vegetable oil, for deep-frying |

1 In a bowl, mix together the flour, chilli, turmeric, baking powder, asafoetida and salt to taste. Pass through a sieve into a large mixing bowl.

2 Add the coarsely-crushed seeds, onion, green chillies and coriander leaves and toss together well. Very gradually mix in enough cold water to make a thick batter surrounding all the ingredients.

3 Heat enough oil in a karai or wok for deep-frying. Drop spoonfuls of the mixture into the hot oil and fry until they are golden brown. Leave enough space to turn the fritters. Drain well and serve hot.

# YOGHURT SOUP

### *Karhi*

Some communities in India add sugar to this soup. When Bhajias are added, it is served as a main dish.

| SERVES 4–6 | ½ tsp chilli powder | 1 tsp cumin seeds |
|---|---|---|
| | ½ tsp turmeric | 3 cloves garlic, crushed |
| **Ingredients** | salt, to taste | 1 piece fresh ginger, 5cm/2in long, crushed |
| 450ml/¾ pint/1½ cups natural (plain) yoghurt, beaten | 2–3 green chillies, finely chopped | 3–4 curry leaves |
| 4 tbsp gram flour (besan) | 4 tbsp vegetable oil | fresh coriander leaves, chopped, to garnish |
| | 4 whole dried red chillies | |

1 Mix together the first 5 ingredients and pass through a strainer into a saucepan. Add the green chillies and cook gently for about 10 minutes, stirring occasionally. Be careful not to let the soup boil over.

2 Heat the oil in a frying pan and fry the remaining spices, garlic and ginger until the dried chillies turn black.

3 Pour the oil and the spices over the yoghurt soup, cover the pan and leave to rest for 5 minutes off the heat. Mix well and gently reheat for a further 5 minutes. Serve hot, garnished with the coriander leaves.

# LENTIL SOUP

### *Dhal Sherva*

This is a simple, mildly spiced lentil soup, which is a good accompaniment to heavily spiced meat dishes.

SERVES 4–6

**Ingredients**
1 tbsp ghee
1 large onion, finely chopped
2 cloves garlic, crushed
1 green chilli, chopped
½ tsp turmeric
85g/3oz red lentils (masoor dhal)

250ml/8fl oz/1 cup water
salt, to taste
400g/14oz canned tomatoes, chopped
½ tsp sugar
lemon juice, to taste
200g/7oz/1 cup plain boiled rice or 2 potatoes,
    boiled (optional)
coriander leaves, chopped, to garnish

1 Heat the ghee in a large saucepan and fry the onion, garlic, chilli and turmeric until the onion is translucent.

2 Add the lentils and water and bring to the boil. Reduce the heat, cover and cook until all the water is absorbed.

3 Mash the lentils with the back of a wooden spoon until you have a smooth paste. Add salt to taste and mix well.

4 Add the remaining ingredients. Reheat the soup and serve hot. To provide extra texture, fold in the plain boiled rice or potatoes cut into small cubes.

### Cook's tip

When using lentils, first rinse in cold water and remove any floating items.

# POTATO CAKES WITH STUFFING

*Petis*

Only a few communities in India make these unusual starters. Petis can also be served as a main meal with Tomato Salad.

| MAKES 7–10 | | |
|---|---|---|
| **Ingredients** | 1 tsp coriander powder | juice of 1 lemon |
| 1 tbsp vegetable oil | 1 tsp cumin powder | 900g/2lb potatoes, boiled and mashed |
| 1 large onion, finely chopped | 2 green chillies, finely chopped | 2 eggs, beaten |
| 2 cloves garlic, finely crushed | 2 tbsp each, chopped coriander and mint leaves | breadcrumbs, for coating |
| 1 piece fresh ginger, 5cm/2in long, finely crushed | 225g/8oz lean minced (ground) beef or lamb | vegetable oil, for shallow-frying |
|  | 50g/2oz frozen peas, thawed | lemon wedges, to serve |
|  | salt, to taste | |

**1** Heat the tbsp of oil and fry the first 7 ingredients until the onion is translucent. Add the meat and peas and fry well until the meat is cooked, then season with salt and lemon juice. The mixture should be very dry.

**2** Divide the mashed potato into 8–10 portions, take a portion and flatten into a pancake in the palm of your hand. Place a spoonful of the meat in the centre and gather the sides together to enclose the meat. Flatten it slightly to make a round shape.

**3** Dip each petis in beaten egg and then coat in breadcrumbs. Allow to chill in the refrigerator for about 1 hour.

**4** Heat the oil in a frying pan and shallow-fry the cakes until all the sides are brown and crisp. Serve hot with lemon wedges.

# SOUTH INDIAN PEPPER WATER

*Tamatar Rasam*

This is a highly soothing broth for winter evenings, also known as Mulla-ga-tani. Serve with the whole spices or strain and reheat if you so wish. The lemon juice may be adjusted to taste, but this dish should be distinctly sour.

**SERVES 4–6**

**Ingredients**
2 tbsp vegetable oil
½ tsp freshly-ground black pepper
I tsp cumin seeds
½ tsp mustard seeds
¼ tsp asafoetida
2 whole dried red chillies
4–6 curry leaves
½ tsp turmeric
2 cloves garlic, crushed
300ml/½ pint/1¼ cups tomato juice
juice of 2 lemons
100ml/4fl oz/½ cup water
salt, to taste
coriander leaves, chopped, to garnish

1 In a large frying pan, heat the oil and fry the next 8 ingredients until the chillies are nearly black and the garlic golden brown.

2 Lower the heat and add the tomato juice, lemon juice, water and salt. Bring to the boil then simmer for 10 minutes. Garnish with the chopped coriander and serve.

---

# CHICKEN MULLIGATAWNY

*Kozhi Mulla-ga-tani*

Using the original Pepper Water – Mulla-ga-tani – this dish was created by the non-vegetarian chefs during the British Raj. The recipe was imported to the United Kingdom and today ranks highly on several restaurant menus as Mulligatawny soup.

**SERVES 4–6**

**Ingredients**
900g/2lb chicken, boned, skinned and cubed
575ml/1 pint/2½ cups water
6 green cardamom pods
I piece cinnamon stick, 5cm/2in long
4–6 curry leaves
I tbsp coriander powder
I tsp cumin powder
½ tsp turmeric
3 cloves garlic, crushed
12 whole peppercorns
4 cloves
I onion, finely chopped
115g/4oz coconut cream block
salt, to taste
juice of 2 lemons
deep-fried onions, to garnish
coriander leaves, chopped, to garnish

1 Place the chicken in a large pan with the water and cook until the chicken is tender. Skim the surface, then strain, reserving the stock and keeping the chicken warm.

2 Return the stock to the pan and reheat. Add all the remaining ingredients, except the chicken, deep-fried onions and coriander. Simmer for 10–15 minutes, then strain and return the chicken to the soup. Reheat, garnish with deep-fried onions and chopped coriander and serve.

# Pastry Triangles with Spicy Filling

*Samosas*

Traditional samosa pastry requires a lot of time and hard work but spring roll pastry makes an excellent substitute and is readily available. One packet will make 30 samosas. They can be frozen before or after frying.

MAKES 30

**Ingredients**
1 packet spring roll pastry, thawed and
    wrapped in a damp towel
vegetable oil, for deep-frying

**Filling**
3 large potatoes, boiled and coarsely mashed
85g/3oz frozen peas, boiled and drained
50g/2oz canned sweetcorn, drained
1 tsp coriander powder
1 tsp cumin powder

1 tsp amchur (dry mango powder)
1 small onion (red if available), finely chopped
salt, to taste
2 green chillies, finely chopped
2 tbsp each, coriander and mint leaves, chopped
juice of 1 lemon

1 Toss all the filling ingredients together in a large mixing bowl until well blended. Adjust seasoning of salt and lemon juice, if necessary.

2 Using one strip of pastry at a time, place 1 tbsp of the filling mixture at one end of the strip and diagonally fold the pastry to form a triangle.

3 Heat enough oil for deep-frying and fry the samosas in small batches until they are golden brown. Serve hot with Fresh Coriander Relish or a chilli sauce.

# Spicy Omelette

*Poro*

Eggs are packed with nutritional value and make wholesome and delicious dishes. This omelette, cooked with potato, onion and a touch of spices, can be put together quickly for an emergency meal.

SERVES 4–6

**Ingredients**
2 tbsp vegetable oil
1 medium onion, finely chopped
½ tsp cumin powder
1 clove garlic, finely crushed
1 or 2 green chillies, finely chopped
a few sprigs fresh coriander, chopped
1 firm tomato, chopped
1 small potato, cubed and boiled
25g/1oz cooked peas
25g/1oz cooked sweetcorn
salt and pepper, to taste
2 eggs, beaten
25g/1oz grated cheese

1 Heat the oil in a saucepan and fry the next 9 ingredients until well blended but the potato and tomato are firm. Season to taste.

2 Increase the heat and pour in the beaten eggs. Reduce the heat, cover and cook until the bottom layer is brown. Turn the omelette over and sprinkle with the grated cheese. Place under a hot grill and cook until the egg sets and the cheese has melted.

# RICE LAYERED WITH CHICKEN AND POTATOES

*Murgh Biryani*

This dish is mainly prepared for important occasions, and is truly fit for royalty. Every cook in India has a subtle variation which is kept a closely-guarded secret.

---

**SERVES 4–6**

**Ingredients**
1.3kg/3lb chicken breast fillet, skinned and cut into
    large pieces
4 tbsp biryani masala paste
2 green chillies, chopped
1 tbsp crushed fresh ginger
1 tbsp crushed garlic
50g/2oz coriander leaves, chopped
6–8 mint leaves, chopped, or 1 tsp mint sauce
150ml/½ pint/⅔ cup natural (plain) yoghurt,
    beaten

2 tbsp tomato purée (paste)
4 onions, finely sliced, deep-fried and crushed
salt, to taste
450g/1lb basmati rice, washed and drained
1 tsp black cumin seeds
1 piece cinnamon stick, 5cm/2in long
4 green cardamoms
2 black cardamoms
vegetable oil, for shallow-frying
4 large potatoes, peeled and quartered
175ml/6fl oz/¾ cup milk, mixed with 85ml/
    3fl oz/⅓ cup water
1 sachet saffron powder, mixed with 6 tbsp milk

2 tbsp ghee or unsalted (sweet) butter

**Garnish**
ghee or unsalted (sweet) butter, for shallow-
    frying
50g/2oz cashew nuts
50g/2oz sultanas (white raisins)
2 hard-boiled eggs, quartered
deep-fried onion slices

---

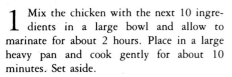

1 Mix the chicken with the next 10 ingredients in a large bowl and allow to marinate for about 2 hours. Place in a large heavy pan and cook gently for about 10 minutes. Set aside.

2 Boil a large pan of water and soak the rice with the cumin seeds, cinnamon stick and green and black cardamoms for about 5 minutes. Drain well. Some of the whole spices may be removed at this stage.

3 Heat the oil for shallow-frying and fry the potatoes until they are evenly browned on all sides. Drain and set aside.

4 Place half the rice on top of the chicken in the pan in an even layer. Then make an even layer with the potatoes. Put the remaining rice on top of the potatoes and spread to make an even layer.

5 Sprinkle the water mixed with milk all over the rice. Make random holes through the rice with the handle of a spoon and pour into each a little saffron milk. Place a few knobs of ghee or butter on the surface, cover and cook over a low heat for 35–45 minutes.

6 While the biryani is cooking, make the garnish. Heat a little ghee or butter and fry the cashew nuts and sultanas (white raisins) until they swell. Drain and set aside. When the biryani is ready, gently toss the rice, chicken and potatoes together, garnish with the nut mixture, hard-boiled eggs and onion slices and serve hot.

# RICE LAYERED WITH PRAWNS (SHRIMP)

*Jingha Gucci Biryani*

This dish makes a meal in itself, requiring only pickles or raitha as an accompaniment. If serving for a party, complete your table with Boiled Egg Curry and Potatoes in a Hot Red Sauce.

**SERVES 4–6**

**Ingredients**

2 large onions, finely sliced and deep fried
300ml/½ pint/1¼ cups natural yoghurt
2 tbsp tomato purée (paste)
4 tbsp green masala paste
2 tbsp lemon juice
salt, to taste
1 tsp black cumin seeds

1 piece cinnamon stick, 5cm/2in long, or ¼ tsp
  cinnamon
4 green cardamoms
450g/1lb fresh king prawns (shrimp), peeled and
  de-veined
225g/8oz small whole button mushrooms
225g/8oz frozen peas, thawed and drained
450g/1lb basmati rice soaked for 5 minutes in
  boiled water and drained
300ml/½ pint/1¼ cups water

1 sachet saffron powder mixed in 6 tbsp milk
2 tbsp ghee or unsalted (sweet) butter

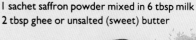

1 Mix the first 9 ingredients together in a large bowl. Fold the prawns (shrimp), mushrooms and peas into the marinade and leave for about 2 hours.

2 Grease the base of a heavy pan and add the prawns (shrimp), vegetables and any marinade juices. Cover with the drained rice and smooth the surface gently until you have an even layer.

3 Pour the water all over the surface of the rice. Make random holes through the rice with the handle of a spoon and pour into each a little saffron milk.

4 Place a few knobs of ghee or butter on the surface and place a circular piece of foil directly on top of the rice. Cover and cook over a low heat for 45–50 minutes. Gently toss the rice, prawns (shrimp) and vegetables together and serve hot.

# Unleavened Bread Roasted with Ghee

## *Paratha*

A richer, softer and flakier variation on chappatis, parathas require longer preparation time so plan your menu well ahead. Like chappatis, parathas can be kept warm wrapped in foil.

MAKES 12–15

water, to mix
50g/2oz atta (wholemeal flour), for dusting

**Ingredients**
350g/12oz atta (wholemeal flour)
50g/2oz plain (all-purpose) flour
salt, to taste
6 tsp ghee
2 tsp ghee, melted

1 Sift the flours and salt into a large mixing bowl. Make a well in the centre and add 2 tsp of the ghee and fold into the flour to make a crumbly texture. Very gradually add enough water to make a soft but pliable dough. Cover and leave to rest for 1 hour.

2 Divide the dough into 12–15 equal portions and keep covered. Take one portion at a time and roll out on a lightly-floured surface to about 10cm/4in in diameter. Brush with a little of the melted ghee and sprinkle with atta. With a sharp knife, make a straight cut from the centre to the edge.

3 Lift a cut edge and roll the dough into a cone shape. Lift it and flatten it again into a ball. Roll the dough again on a floured surface until it is 17.5cm/7in wide.

4 Heat a griddle and cook one paratha at a time, placing a little of the remaining ghee along the edges. Cook on each side until golden brown. Serve hot.

# ROASTED UNLEAVENED BREAD

### *Chappati*

Chappatis are prepared daily in most Indian homes. They are best eaten as soon as they are cooked although they can be kept warm, wrapped in foil and placed in a warm oven.

| MAKES 10–12 | 1 tsp salt | ghee or unsalted (sweet) butter, for spreading |
| --- | --- | --- |
| **Ingredients** | water, to mix | |
| 350g/12oz atta (wholemeal flour) | a few drops of vegetable oil, for brushing | |
| | 50g/2oz atta (wholemeal flour), for dusting | |

1 Sift the flour and salt into a large bowl. Make a well in the centre and slowly add small quantities of water until you have a smooth but pliable dough. Grease the palms of your hands and knead the dough well. Keep covered until you are ready to use.

2 Divide the dough into 10–12 equal portions, using one portion at a time and keeping the rest covered. Knead each portion into a ball, then flatten with your hands and place on a floured surface. Roll out until you have a circle about 17.5cm/7in in diameter.

3 Heat a heavy griddle and, when hot, roast the chappatis on each side, pressing the edges down gently. When both sides are ready, brush the first side lightly with ghee or butter.

# LEAVENED BREAD

### *Naan*

Traditionally, naans are baked in a tandoor or clay oven, though grilled naans look just as authentic.

| MAKES 6–8 | 450g/1lb plain (all-purpose) flour | 1 egg, beaten |
| --- | --- | --- |
| | 1 tsp baking powder | 25g/1oz melted ghee |
| **Ingredients** | ½ tsp salt | flour, for dusting |
| 2 tsp dry active yeast | 150ml/¼ pint/⅔ cup milk | ghee, for greasing |
| 4 tbsp warm milk | 150ml/¼ pint/⅔ cup natural (plain) yoghurt, | chopped coriander leaves and onion seeds, to |
| 2 tsp sugar | beaten | sprinkle |

1 Mix the yeast, warm milk and sugar and leave to become frothy. Sift the flour, baking powder and salt. Make a well in the centre and add the yeast mixture, milk, yoghurt, egg and ghee. Fold in all the ingredients.

2 Knead the dough well. Tightly cover the bowl and keep in a warm place until the dough doubles. To test, push a finger into the dough – it should spring back. Roll out the dough on a floured surface.

3 Make each naan slipper-shaped, about 25cm/10in long and about 15cm/6in wide, tapering to 5cm/2in. Sprinkle with the coriander and onion seeds. Place on greased trays and bake at 200°C/400°F/Gas Mark 6.

# PLAIN BOILED RICE

## *Chawal*

In India, rice is consumed in great quantities by all members of society. There are numerous ways in which it can be prepared, but plain boiled rice is the most common.

SERVES 4–6

**Ingredients**
1 tbsp ghee, unsalted (sweet) butter or olive oil

350g/12oz basmati rice, washed and drained
500ml/¾ pint/2 cups water
salt, to taste

### Cook's tip

To make Kesar Chawal or fragrant rice, sauté 4–6 green cardamoms, 4 cloves, 5cm/2in piece cinnamon stick, ½ tsp black cumin seeds and 2 bay leaves. Add 350g/12oz drained basmati rice and proceed as for plain boiled rice. For an even more luxurious rice, add 6–8 strands of saffron and sauté with the spices.

1 Heat the ghee, butter or oil in a saucepan and sauté the drained rice thoroughly for about 2–3 minutes.

2 Add the water and salt and bring to the boil. Reduce the heat to low, cover and cook gently for 15–20 minutes. To serve, fluff the grains gently with a fork.

# FRAGRANT RICE WITH MEAT

## *Yakhni Pilau*

This rice dish acquires its delicious taste from not only the spices but the richly flavoured meat stock.

SERVES 4–6

**Ingredients**
900g/2lb chicken pieces, or lean lamb, cubed
575ml/1 pint/2½ cups water
4 green cardamoms

2 black cardamoms
10 whole peppercorns
4 cloves
1 medium onion, sliced
salt, to taste
450g/1lb basmati rice, washed and drained

8–10 saffron strands
2 cloves garlic, crushed
1 piece fresh ginger, 5cm/2in long, crushed
1 piece cinnamon stick, 5cm/2in long
175g/6oz sultanas (white raisins) and peeled almonds, sautéed, to garnish

1 In a large saucepan, cook the chicken or lamb in the water with the cardamoms, peppercorns, cloves, onion and salt until the meat is cooked. Remove the meat and keep warm. Strain the stock if you wish, and return to the saucepan.

2 Add the rice, saffron, garlic, ginger and cinnamon to the stock and bring the contents to the boil.

3 Quickly add the meat and stir well. Bring back to the boil, reduce the heat and cover. Cook covered for about 15–20 minutes. Remove from the heat for 5 minutes. Add the contents of the saucepan. Garnish with sultanas (white raisins) and almonds and serve.

# RICE LAYERED WITH LENTILS AND GOURD CURRY

## *Dhal Chawal Palida*

Bhori Muslims in India have their own special style of cooking and have adapted many of the traditional dishes from other Indian communities. Palida is prominently flavoured with fenugreek and soured with kokum (dried mangosteen). Lemon juice will provide the same effect.

SERVES 4–6

**Ingredients**
175g/6oz bengal gram
575ml/1 pint/2½ cups water
½ tsp turmeric powder
50g/2oz deep-fried onions, crushed
3 tbsp green masala paste
a few mint and coriander leaves, chopped
salt, to taste
350g/12oz basmati rice, cooked
2 tbsp ghee

a little water
4 tbsp vegetable oil
¼ tsp fenugreek seeds
15g/½oz dried fenugreek leaves
2 cloves garlic, crushed
1 tsp coriander powder
1 tsp cumin seeds
1 tsp chilli powder
4 tbsp gram flour mixed with 4 tbsp water
450g/1lb bottle gourd peeled, pith and seeds removed and cut into bite-size pieces or marrow (squash) or firm courgettes (zucchini)

175ml/6fl oz/¾ cup tomato juice
6 kokum (dried mangosteen), or juice of 3 lemons
salt, to taste
coriander leaves, to garnish

1 For the rice, boil the bengal gram in the water with the turmeric until the grains are soft but not mushy. Drain and reserve the water for the curry.

2 Toss the bengal gram gently with the deep-fried onions, green masala paste, chopped mint and coriander leaves, and salt.

3 Grease a heavy pan and place a layer of rice in the bottom. Add the bengal gram mixture and another layer of the remaining rice. Place small knobs of ghee on top, sprinkle with a little water and gently heat until steam gathers in the pan.

4 To make the curry, heat the oil in a pan and fry the fenugreek seeds and leaves and garlic until the garlic turns golden brown.

5 Mix the spice powders to a paste with a little water. Add to the pan and simmer until all the water evaporates.

6 Add the remaining ingredients, and cook until the gourd is soft and transparent. Garnish with the coriander leaves and serve hot with Dhal Chawal.

# MOGHUL-STYLE ROAST LAMB

*Shahi Raan*

This superb dish is just one of many fine examples of fabulous rich food once enjoyed by Moghul Emperors. Try it as a variation to roast beef.

SERVES 4–6

**Ingredients**
4 large onions, chopped
4 cloves garlic
1 piece fresh ginger, 5cm/2in long chopped
3 tbsp ground almonds
2 tsp cumin powder
2 tsp coriander powder
2 tsp turmeric

2 tsp garam masala
4–6 green chillies
juice of 1 lemon
salt, to taste
300ml/½ pint/1¼ cups natural (plain) yoghurt, beaten
1.8kg/4lb leg of lamb
8–10 cloves
4 firm tomatoes, halved and grilled, to serve
1 tbsp blanched almond flakes, to garnish

1 Place the first 11 ingredients in a food processor and blend to a smooth paste. Gradually add the yoghurt and blend. Grease a large, deep baking tray and preheat the oven to 190°C/375°F/Gas Mark 5.

2 Remove most of the fat and skin from the lamb. Using a sharp knife, make deep pockets above the bone at each side of the thick end. Make deep diagonal gashes on both sides.

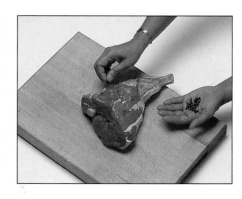

3 Push the cloves into the meat at random.

4 Push some of the spice mixture into the pockets and gashes and spread the remainder evenly all over the meat.

5 Place the meat on the baking tray and loosely cover the whole tray with foil. Roast for 2–2½ hours or until the meat is cooked, removing the foil for the last 10 minutes of cooking time.

6 Remove from the oven and allow to rest for 10 minutes before carving. Serve with grilled tomatoes and garnish the joint with almond flakes.

# KASHMIRI-STYLE LAMB

### *Rogan Josh*

This curry originated in Kashmir, and derives its name from the large quantities of red chillies used in the dish. They may be reduced for a milder flavour, with paprika and 2 tsp tomato purée (paste) added to retain the colour.

| SERVES 4–6 | 900g/2lb lean lamb, cubed | 8–10 strands saffron (optional) |
|---|---|---|
| | 1 piece fresh ginger, 5cm/2in long, crushed | salt, to taste |
| **Ingredients** | 2 cloves garlic, crushed | 150ml/¼ pint/⅔ cup natural (plain) yoghurt, |
| 4 tbsp vegetable oil | 4 tbsp rogan josh masala paste | beaten |
| ¼ tsp asafoetida | 1 tsp chilli powder or 2 tsp sweet paprika | blanched almond flakes, to garnish |

1 Heat the oil in a frying pan and fry the asafoetida and lamb, stirring well to seal the meat. Reduce the heat, cover and cook for about 10 minutes.

2 Add the remaining ingredients except the yoghurt and almonds and mix well. If the meat is too dry, add a very small quantity of boiling water. Cover and cook on a low heat for a further 10 minutes.

3 Remove the pan from the heat and leave to cool a little. Add the yoghurt, 1 tbsp at a time, stirring constantly to avoid curdling. Cook uncovered on low until the gravy becomes thick. Garnish and serve hot.

# HOT DRY MEAT CURRY

### *Sookha Gosht*

This dish is nearly as hot as phaal (India's hottest curry), but the spices can still be distinguished above the chilli.

| SERVES 4–6 | 4 cloves garlic, crushed | 1 tsp turmeric |
|---|---|---|
| | 6–8 curry leaves | salt, to taste |
| **Ingredients** | 3 tbsp extra hot curry paste, or 4 tbsp hot curry | 900g/2lb lean lamb, beef or pork, cubed |
| 2 tbsp vegetable oil | powder | 175ml/6fl oz/¾ cup thick coconut milk |
| 1 large onion, finely sliced | 3 tsp chilli powder | 2 large tomatoes, finely chopped, to garnish |
| 1 piece fresh ginger, 5cm/2in long, crushed | 1 tsp five-spice powder | |

1 Heat the oil and fry the onion, ginger, garlic and curry leaves until the onion is soft. Add the curry paste, chilli and five-spice powder, turmeric and salt.

2 Add the meat and stir well over a medium heat to seal and evenly brown the meat pieces. Keep stirring until the oil separates. Cover and cook for about 20 minutes.

3 Add the coconut milk, mix well and simmer until the meat is cooked. Towards the end of cooking, uncover the pan to reduce the excess liquid. Garnish and serve hot.

# SPICY MEAT LOAF

*Lagan Ki Seekh*

This mixture is baked in the oven and provides a hearty breakfast on cold winter mornings.

| SERVES 4–6 | 2 tbsp finely-ground ginger | 50g/2oz coriander leaves, chopped |
|---|---|---|
| | 2 tbsp finely-ground garlic | 175g/6oz potato, grated |
| **Ingredients** | 6 green chillies, chopped | salt, to taste |
| 5 eggs | 2 small onions, finely chopped | |
| 450g/1lb lean minced (ground) beef | ½ tsp turmeric |  |

1 Preheat the oven to 180°C/350°F/Gas Mark 4. Beat 2 eggs until fluffy and pour into a greased baking tray.

2 Knead the meat, ginger and garlic, 4 green chillies, 1 chopped onion, 1 beaten egg, the turmeric, coriander leaves, potato and salt. Pack into the baking tray and smooth the surface. Cook for 45 minutes.

3 Beat the remaining eggs and fold in the remaining green chillies and onion. Remove the baking tray from the oven and pour the mixture all over the meat. Return to the oven and cook until the eggs have set.

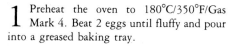

# SPICY KEBABS

*Kofta*

Serve these tasty kebabs piping hot with Leavened Bread, Raitha and Tomato Salad.
Leftover kebabs can be coarsely chopped and packed into pitta bread spread with Fresh Coriander Relish.

| MAKES 20–25 | 4 green chillies, finely chopped | 4–6 mint leaves, chopped, or ½ tsp mint sauce |
|---|---|---|
| | 1 small onion, finely chopped | 175g/6oz raw potato |
| **Ingredients** | 1 egg | salt, to taste |
| 450g/1lb lean minced (ground) beef or lamb | ½ tsp turmeric | vegetable oil, for deep-frying |
| 2 tbsp finely-ground ginger | 1 tsp garam masala |  |
| 2 tbsp finely-ground garlic | 50g/2oz coriander leaves, chopped | |

1 Place the first 10 ingredients in a large bowl. Grate the potato into the bowl, and season with salt. Knead together to blend well and form a soft dough.

2 Shape the mixture into portions the size of golf balls. Leave to rest for about 25 minutes.

3 In a wok or frying pan, heat the oil to medium-hot and fry the koftas in small batches until they are golden brown in colour. Drain well and serve hot.

# MINCE KEBABS

*Shammi Kebab*

Serve this Indian hamburger in a bun with chilli sauce and salad or unaccompanied as a starter.

SERVES 4–6

**Ingredients**
2 onions, finely chopped
250g/9oz lean lamb, cut into small cubes
50g/2oz bengal gram
1 tsp cumin seeds
1 tsp garam masala
4–6 green chillies
1 piece fresh ginger, 5cm/2in long, crushed
salt, to taste
175ml/6fl oz/¾ cup water
a few coriander and mint leaves, chopped
juice of 1 lemon
1 tbsp gram flour
2 eggs, beaten
vegetable oil, for shallow-frying

1 Put the first 8 ingredients and the water into a pan and bring to the boil. Simmer, covered, until the meat and dhal are cooked. Cook uncovered to reduce the excess liquid. Cool, and grind to a paste.

2 Place the mixture in a mixing bowl and add the coriander and mint leaves, lemon juice and gram flour. Knead well. Divide into 10–12 portions and roll each into a ball, then flatten slightly. Chill for 1 hour. Dip the kebabs in the beaten egg and shallow-fry each side until golden brown. Serve hot.

# CURRIED MINCE

*Kheema*

This can be served as a main dish or mixed with fried or scrambled eggs for a brunch. It also makes a good pizza topping.

SERVES 4–6

**Ingredients**
1 tsp vegetable oil
1 large onion, finely chopped
2 cloves garlic, crushed
1 piece fresh ginger, 5cm/2in long, crushed
4 green chillies, chopped
2 tbsp curry powder
450g/1lb lean minced (ground) beef, or lamb
225g/8oz frozen peas, thawed
salt, to taste
juice of 1 lemon
a few coriander leaves, chopped

1 Fry the onion, garlic, ginger and chillies until the onion is translucent. Lower the heat, add the curry powder and mix well.

2 Add the meat and stir well, pressing the meat down with the back of a spoon. Add the peas, salt and lemon juice, mix well, cover and simmer. Fold in the coriander. Serve hot.

# PORTUGUESE PORK

*Soovar Vindaloo*

This dish displays the influence of Portuguese cooking on Indian cuisine.

SERVES 4–6

**Ingredients**
115g/4oz deep-fried onions, crushed
4 red chillies, or 1 tsp chilli powder
4 tbsp vindaloo masala paste
6 tbsp white wine vinegar
6 tbsp tomato purée (paste)
½ tsp fenugreek seeds
1 tsp turmeric
1 tsp crushed mustard seeds, or ½ tsp mustard powder
salt, to taste
1½ tsp sugar
900g/2lb boneless pork spareribs, cubed
1 cup water
plain boiled rice, to serve

1 Place all the ingredients except the water and rice in a heavy steel pan or mixing bowl and mix well. Marinate for about 2 hours

2 Add the water and mix well. Simmer gently for about 2 hours. Adjust the seasoning. Serve hot with the plain boiled rice.

# STEAK AND KIDNEY WITH SPINACH

*Sag Gosht*

When this dish is cooked in India, the spinach is often pulverized. Here, it is coarsely chopped and added in the last stages of cooking, which retains the nutritional value of the spinach and gives the dish a lovely appearance.

**SERVES 4–6**

**Ingredients**
2 tbsp vegetable oil
1 large onion, finely chopped
1 piece fresh ginger, 5cm/2in long, crushed
4 cloves garlic, crushed
4 tbsp mild curry paste, or 4 tbsp mild
   curry powder

¼ tsp turmeric
salt, to taste
900g/2lb steak and kidney, cubed
450g/1lb fresh spinach, trimmed, washed
   and chopped or 450g/1lb frozen spinach,
   thawed and drained
4 tbsp tomato purée (paste)
2 large tomatoes, finely chopped

**1** Heat the oil in a frying pan and fry the onion, ginger and garlic until the onion is soft and the ginger and garlic turn golden brown.

**2** Lower the heat and add the curry paste or powder, turmeric, salt and meat and mix well. Cover and cook until the meat is nearly tender.

**3** Add the spinach and tomato purée (paste) and mix well. Cook uncovered until the spinach is softened and most of the liquid evaporated.

**4** Fold in the chopped tomatoes. Increase the heat and cook for about 5 minutes.

# MADRAS

*Madras Attu Erachi*

This popular South Indian curry is mainly prepared by Muslims and is traditionally made with beef.

| SERVES 4–6 | 4 green cardamoms | 450g/1lb lean beef, cubed |
|---|---|---|
| | 2 whole star anise | 4 tbsp tamarind juice |
| **Ingredients** | 4 green chillies, chopped | salt, to taste |
| 4 tbsp vegetable oil | 2 red chillies, chopped (fresh or dried) | sugar, to taste |
| 1 large onion, finely sliced | 3 tbsp madras masala paste | a few coriander leaves, chopped, to garnish |
| 3–4 cloves | 1 tsp turmeric | |

1 Heat the oil in a frying pan and fry the onion until it is golden brown. Lower the heat and add all the spice ingredients and fry for a further 2–3 minutes.

2 Add the beef and mix well. Cover and cook on low heat until the beef is tender. Cook uncovered on a higher heat for the last few minutes to reduce any excess liquid.

3 Fold in the tamarind juice, salt and sugar. Reheat the dish and serve hot, garnished with the chopped coriander leaves.

# LAMB IN A CREAMY SAUCE

*Korma*

This is a creamy, aromatic dish with no 'hot' taste. It comes from the kitchens of the Nizam of Hyderabad.

| SERVES 4–6 | 6 cloves garlic, sliced | 900g/2lb lean lamb, cubed |
|---|---|---|
| | 1 piece fresh ginger, 5cm/2in long, sliced | 1 tsp cumin powder |
| **Ingredients** | 1 onion, finely chopped | 1 tsp coriander powder |
| 1 tbsp white sesame seeds | 3 tbsp ghee or vegetable oil | salt, to taste |
| 1 tbsp white poppy seeds | 6 green cardamoms | 300ml/½ pint/1¼ cups double (heavy) cream |
| 50g/2oz almonds, blanched | 1 piece cinnamon stick, 5cm/2in long | mixed with ½ tsp cornflour (cornstarch) |
| 2 green chillies, seeded | 4 cloves | roasted sesame seeds, to garnish |

1 Heat a frying pan without any liquid and dry-roast the first 7 ingredients. Cool the mixture and grind to a fine paste using a pestle and mortar or food processor. Heat the ghee or oil in a frying pan.

2 Fry the cardamoms, cinnamon and cloves until the cloves swell. Add the lamb, cumin and coriander powders and the prepared paste, and season. Cover and cook until the lamb is almost done.

3 Remove from the heat, cool a little and gradually fold in the cream, reserving 1 tsp to garnish. To serve, gently reheat the lamb uncovered and serve hot, garnished with the sesame seeds and the remaining cream.

# TANDOORI CHICKEN

*Tandoori Murgh*

This is probably the most famous of Indian dishes. Marinate the chicken well and cook in an extremely hot oven for a clay-oven-baked taste. If you wish authentic 'burnt' spots on the chicken, place the dish under a hot grill for a few minutes after cooking.

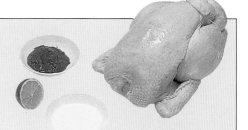

| SERVES 4–6 | 4 tbsp tandoori masala paste |
| --- | --- |
| | salt, to taste |
| **Ingredients** | 85g/3oz ghee |
| 1.3kg/3lb ready-to-roast chicken | lettuce, to serve |
| 225ml/8oz/1 cup natural (plain) yoghurt, beaten | lemon wedges and onion rings, to garnish |

1 Using a sharp knife or scissors, remove the skin from the chicken and trim off any excess fat. Using a fork, beat the flesh at random.

2 Cut the chicken in half down the centre and through the breast. Cut each piece in half again. Make a few deep gashes diagonally into the flesh. Mix the yoghurt with the masala paste and salt. Spread the chicken evenly with the yoghurt mixture, spreading some into the gashes. Leave for at least 2 hours, but preferably overnight.

3 Place the chicken quarters on a wire rack in a deep baking tray. Spread the chicken with any excess marinade, reserve a little for basting halfway through cooking time.

4 Melt the ghee and pour over the chicken to seal the surface. This helps to keep the centre moist during the roasting period. Cook in the oven for 10 minutes at maximum heat, then remove, leaving the oven on.

5 Baste the chicken pieces with the remaining marinade. Return to the oven and switch off the heat. Leave the chicken in the oven for about 15–20 minutes without opening the door. Serve on a bed of lettuce and garnish with the lemon and onion rings.

# STUFFED ROAST CHICKEN

*Murgh Mussallam*

At one time, this dish was only cooked in royal palaces and ingredients varied according to individual chefs. The saffron and rich stuffing make it a truly royal dish.

SERVES 4–6

**Ingredients**
1 sachet saffron powder
½ tsp ground nutmeg
1 tbsp warm milk
1.3kg/3lb whole chicken
6 tbsp ghee
75ml/5 tbsp/⅓ cup hot water

**Stuffing**
3 medium onions, finely chopped
2 green chillies, chopped

50g/2oz sultanas (white raisins)
50g/2oz ground almonds
50g/2oz dried apricots, soaked until soft
3 hard-boiled eggs, coarsely chopped
salt, to taste

**Masala**
4 spring onions (scallions), chopped
2 cloves garlic, crushed
1 tsp five-spice powder
4–6 green cardamoms
½ tsp turmeric
1 tsp freshly-ground black pepper

2 tbsp natural (plain) yoghurt
50g/2oz desiccated (shredded) coconut

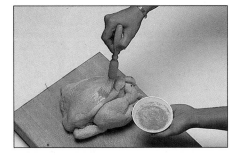

1 Mix together the saffron, nutmeg and milk. Brush the inside of the chicken with the mixture and carefully spread some under the skin. Heat 4 tbsp of the ghee in a large frying pan or wok and fry the chicken on all sides to seal it. Remove and keep warm.

2 To make the stuffing, in the same ghee, fry the onions, chillies, and sultanas (white raisins) for 2–3 minutes. Remove from the heat, allow to cool and add the ground almonds, apricots, chopped eggs and salt. Toss the mixture well, then stuff the chicken.

3 Heat the remaining ghee in a large heavy pan and gently fry all the masala ingredients except the coconut for 2–3 minutes. Add the water. Place the chicken on the bed of masala, cover the pan and cook until the chicken is tender. Set aside keeping warm.

4 Return the pan to the heat and cook to reduce excess fluids in the masala. When the mixture thickens, pour over the chicken. Sprinkle with toasted coconut and serve hot.

# CHICKEN CURRY

*Murgh Ka Salan*

Chicken curry is always popular when served at a family dinner or banquet. This version is cooked covered, giving a thin consistency. If you would prefer it thick, cook uncovered for the last 15 minutes.

**SERVES 4–6**

**Ingredients**
4 tbsp vegetable oil
4 cloves
4–6 green cardamoms
1 piece cinnamon stick, 5cm/2in long
3 whole star anise
6–8 curry leaves
1 large onion, finely chopped
1 piece fresh ginger, 5cm/2in long, crushed
4 cloves garlic, crushed
4 tbsp mild curry paste
1 tsp turmeric
1 tsp five-spice powder
1.3kg/3lb chicken, skinned and jointed
400g/14oz canned tomatoes, chopped
115g/4oz creamed coconut
½ tsp sugar
salt, to taste
50g/2oz coriander leaves, chopped

1 Heat the oil in a frying pan and fry the cloves, cardamoms, cinnamon stick, star anise and curry leaves until the cloves swell and the curry leaves are slightly burnt.

2 Add the onion, ginger and garlic and fry until the onion turns brown. Add the curry paste, turmeric and five-spice powder and fry until the oil separates.

3 Add the chicken pieces and mix well. When all the pieces are evenly sealed, cover and cook until the meat is nearly done.

4 Add the chopped tomatoes and the creamed coconut. Simmer gently until the coconut dissolves. Mix well and add the sugar and salt. Fold in the coriander leaves, reheat and serve hot.

# BOILED EGG CURRY

*Andoan Ka Salan*

This dish is usually served with biryani or pilau but it is equally good with Fried Whole Fish.

| SERVES 4–6 | 350ml/12fl oz/1½ cups tomato juice | 6 hard-boiled eggs, halved |
|---|---|---|
| **Ingredients** | 2 tsp gram flour (besan) | 2 tbsp sesame oil |
| 2 tsp white poppy seeds | 1 tsp finely-crushed fresh ginger | 1 tsp cumin seeds |
| 2 tsp white sesame seeds | 1 tsp chilli powder | 4 whole dried red chillies |
| 2 tsp whole coriander seeds | ¼ tsp asafoetida | 6–8 curry leaves |
| 2 tbsp desiccated (shredded) coconut | salt, to taste | 4 cloves garlic, finely sliced |
| | 1 tsp sugar | |

**1** Heat a frying pan and dry-fry the poppy, sesame and coriander seeds for 3–4 minutes. Add the desiccated (shredded) coconut and dry-fry until it browns. Cool and grind the ingredients together using a pestle and mortar or a food processor.

**2** Take a little of the tomato juice and mix with the gram flour (besan) to a smooth paste. Add the ginger, chilli powder, asafoetida, salt and sugar and the ground spices. Add the remaining tomato juice, place in a saucepan and simmer gently for 10 minutes.

**3** Add the hard-boiled eggs and cover with the gravy. Heat the oil in a frying pan and fry the remaining ingredients until the chillies turn dark brown. Pour the spices and oil over the egg curry, fold the ingredients together and reheat. Serve hot.

# EGGS BAKED ON CHIPSTICKS

*Sali Pur Eeda*

Parsis love eggs, and have developed a variety of unique egg-based dishes such as this one.

| SERVES 4–6 | 2 green chillies, finely chopped | 75ml/5 tbsp/⅓ cup water |
|---|---|---|
| | a few coriander leaves, finely chopped | 6 eggs |
| **Ingredients** | ¼ tsp turmeric | salt and freshly-ground black pepper, to taste |
| 225g/8oz ready-salted chipsticks | 4 tbsp vegetable oil | 3 sprigs spring onions (scallions), finely chopped |

**1** In a bowl, mix the chipsticks, chillies, coriander and turmeric. Heat 2 tbsp of the oil in a frying pan. Add the chipstick mixture and water. Cook until the chipsticks have softened, then fry until crisp.

**2** Place a plate over the frying pan, turn the pan over and remove the chipstick pancake onto it. Reheat the remaining oil in the pan and slide the pancake back to the frying pan to brown the other side.

**3** Gently break the eggs over the pancake, cover the frying pan and allow the eggs to set over a low heat. Season and sprinkle with the spring onions (scallions). Cook until the base is crisp. Serve hot.

# MOGHUL-STYLE CHICKEN

*Moghlai Murgh*

This delicate curry can be served as a starter followed by stronger curries and rice. Saffron is crucial to the dish, but as it is very expensive prepare it for special occasions.

SERVES 4–6

**Ingredients**
2 eggs, beaten with salt and pepper
4 chicken breasts, rubbed with a little garam
    masala
6 tbsp ghee
1 large onion, finely chopped
1 piece fresh ginger, 5cm/2in long, finely crushed
4 cloves garlic, finely crushed

4 cloves
4 green cardamoms
1 piece cinnamon stick, 5cm/2in long
2 bay leaves
15–20 strands of saffron
150ml/¼ pint/⅔ cup natural (plain) yoghurt,
    beaten with 1 tsp cornflour (cornstarch)
salt, to taste
75ml/5 tbsp/⅓ cup double (heavy) cream
50g/2oz ground almonds

1 Brush the chicken breasts with the beaten eggs. In a frying pan, heat the ghee and fry the chicken. Remove and keep warm.

2 In the same ghee, fry the onion, ginger, garlic, cloves, cardamoms, cinnamon and bay leaves. When the onion turns golden, remove the pan from the heat, allow to cool a little and add the saffron and yoghurt. Mix well to prevent the yoghurt from curdling.

3 Return the chicken mixture to the pan with any juices and gently cook until the chicken is tender. Adjust the seasoning if necessary.

4 Just before serving, fold in the cream and ground almonds. Serve hot.

# CHICKEN IN A HOT RED SAUCE

*Kashmiri Murgh*

In India, small chickens are used for this dish and served as an individual starter with Unleavened Bread. If you wish to serve it as a starter, use 4 poussins instead of chicken joints. Skin them first and make small gashes with a sharp knife to enable the spices to seep in.

**SERVES 4–6**

**Ingredients**

4 tsp kashmiri masala paste
4 tbsp tomato sauce (ketchup)
1 tsp Worcestershire sauce
1 tsp five-spice powder
salt, to taste

1 tsp sugar
8 chicken joints, skinned but not boned
3 tbsp vegetable oil
1 fresh piece ginger, 5cm/2in long, finely shredded
4 cloves garlic, finely crushed
juice of 1 lemon
a few coriander leaves, finely chopped

1 To make the marinade, mix together the kashmiri masala, tomato sauce (ketchup), Worcestershire sauce, five-spice powder, salt and sugar. Allow to rest in a warm place until the sugar has dissolved.

2 Rub the chicken pieces with the marinade and allow to rest for a further 2 hours, or overnight if possible.

3 Heat the oil in a frying pan and fry half the ginger and all the garlic until golden brown. Add the chicken pieces, and fry without overlapping until both sides are sealed. Cover and cook until the chicken is nearly tender and the gravy clings with the oil separating.

4 Sprinkle the chicken with the lemon juice, remaining ginger and coriander leaves. Mix well, reheat and serve hot.

# CHICKEN IN SPICY ONIONS

*Murgh Do Piyaza*

This is one of the few dishes of India in which onions appear prominently. Chunky onion slices infused with toasted cumin seeds and shredded ginger add a delicious contrast to the flavour of the chicken.

SERVES 4–6

**Ingredients**
1.3kg/3lb chicken, jointed and skinned
½ tsp turmeric
½ tsp chilli powder
salt, to taste
4 tbsp oil

4 small onions, finely chopped
175g/6oz coriander leaves, coarsely chopped
1 piece fresh ginger, 5cm/2in long, finely shredded
2 green chillies, finely chopped
2 tsp cumin seeds, dry-roasted
75ml/5 tbsp/⅓ cup natural (plain) yoghurt
75ml/5 tbsp/⅓ cup double (heavy) cream
½ tsp cornflour (cornstarch)

1 Rub the chicken joints with the turmeric, chilli powder and salt. Heat the oil in a frying pan and fry the chicken pieces without overlapping until both sides are sealed. Remove and keep warm.

2 Reheat the oil and fry 3 of the chopped onions, 150g/5oz of the coriander leaves, half the ginger, the green chillies and the cumin seeds until the onions are translucent. Return the chicken to the pan with any juices and mix well. Cover and cook gently for 15 minutes.

3 Remove the pan from the heat and allow to cool a little. Mix together the yoghurt, cream and cornflour (cornstarch) and gradually fold into the chicken, mixing well.

4 Return the pan to the heat and gently cook until the chicken is tender. Just before serving, stir in the reserved onion, coriander and ginger. Serve hot.

# HOT SWEET AND SOUR DUCK CASSEROLE

*Dekchi Badak*

This recipe can be made with any game bird, or even rabbit. It is a distinctively sweet, sour and hot dish best eaten with rice as an accompaniment.

**SERVES 4–6**

**Ingredients**
1.3kg/3lb duck, jointed and skinned
4 bay leaves
3 tbsp salt
75ml/5 tbsp/⅓ cup vegetable oil
juice of 5 lemons

8 medium-sized onions, finely chopped
50g/2oz garlic, crushed
50g/2oz chilli powder
300ml/½ pint/1¼ cups pickling vinegar
115g/4oz fresh ginger, finely sliced or shredded
115g/4oz/½ cup sugar
50g/2oz garam masala

1 Place the duck, bay leaves and salt in a large pan and cover with cold water. Bring to the boil then simmer until the duck is fully cooked. Remove the pieces of duck and keep warm. Reserve the liquid as a base for stock or soups.

2 In a large pan, heat the oil and lemon juice until it reaches smoking point. Add the onions, garlic and chilli powder and fry the onions until they are golden brown.

3 Add the vinegar, ginger and sugar and simmer until the sugar dissolves and the oil has separated from the masala.

4 Return the duck to the pan and add the garam masala. Mix well, then reheat until the masala clings to the pieces of duck and the gravy is thick. Adjust the seasoning if necessary. If you prefer a thinner gravy, add a little of the reserved stock.

# BOMBAY DUCK PICKLE

*Bomil Achar*

This unusual fish is found off the west coast of India during the monsoon season. It is salted and dried in the sun and is characterized by a strong smell and distinctive piquancy. How this fish acquired the name Bombay Duck in the Western world still remains a mystery!

**SERVES 4–6**

**Ingredients**
6–8 pieces bomil (Bombay duck),
   soaked in water for 5 minutes
4 tbsp vegetable oil
2 fresh red chillies, crushed
1 tbsp sugar
450g/1lb cherry tomatoes, halved
115g/4oz deep-fried onions

1 Pat the soaked fish dry with kitchen paper. Heat the oil in a frying pan and fry the Bombay duck pieces for about 30–45 seconds on both sides until crisp. Be careful not to burn them as they will taste bitter. Drain well on kitchen paper. When cool, break the fish into small pieces.

2 In the same oil, cook the remaining ingredients until the tomatoes become pulpy and the onions are blended into a gravy. Fold in the Bombay duck pieces and serve hot or cold.

---

# FISH CAKES

*Macchli Kebabs*

Kebabs are usually thought to be made with meat or chicken. These tasty fish kebabs can be made slightly larger and served as fish burgers, or made into small balls served as cocktail snacks.

**MAKES 20**

**Ingredients**
450g/1lb skinned haddock, coley or cod
2 medium potatoes, peeled, boiled and mashed

4 spring onions (scallions), finely chopped
4 green chillies, finely chopped
1 piece fresh ginger, 5cm/2in long, finely crushed
a few coriander and mint leaves, chopped
salt and freshly-ground black pepper, to taste

2 eggs
breadcrumbs, for coating
vegetable oil, for shallow-frying
chilli sauce or sweet chutney, to serve

1 Place the fish in a lightly greased steamer and steam until cooked. Remove but leave on the steaming tray to cool.

2 When the fish is cool, crumble it coarsely into a large bowl and mix in the potatoes, spring onions (scallions), spices, coriander and mint, seasonings and 1 egg.

3 Shape into cakes. Beat the remaining egg and dip the cakes in it, then coat with the breadcrumbs. Heat the oil and fry the rissoles until brown on all sides.

# PRAWNS (SHRIMP) AND FISH IN HERB SAUCE

*Haré Masalé Me Jingha Aur Macchi*

Bengalis are famous for their seafood dishes and always use mustard oil in recipes because it imparts a unique taste, flavour and aroma. No feast in Bengal is complete without one of these celebrated fish dishes.

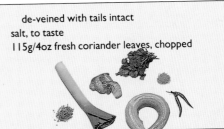

SERVES 4–6

**Ingredients**
3 cloves garlic
1 piece fresh ginger, 5cm/2in long
1 large leek, roughly chopped
4 green chillies
1 tsp vegetable oil (optional)

4 tbsp mustard oil, or vegetable oil
1 tbsp coriander powder
½ tsp fennel seeds
1 tbsp crushed yellow mustard seeds, or 1 tsp mustard powder
175ml/6fl oz/¾ cup thick coconut milk
225g/8oz huss, skate blobs or monkfish
225g/8oz fresh king prawns (shrimp), peeled and

de-veined with tails intact
salt, to taste
115g/4oz fresh coriander leaves, chopped

1 In a food processor, grind the garlic, ginger, leek and chillies to a coarse paste. Add vegetable oil if the mixture is too dry.

2 In a frying pan, heat the mustard or vegetable oil with the paste until it is well blended. Keep the window open and take care not to overheat the mixture as any smoke from the mustard oil will sting the eyes.

3 Add the coriander powder, fennel seeds, mustard and coconut milk. Gently bring to the boil and then simmer, uncovered, for about 5 minutes.

4 Add the fish and simmer for 2 minutes then fold in the prawns (shrimp) and cook until the prawns (shrimp) turn a bright orange/pink colour. Season with salt, fold in the coriander leaves and serve hot.

# PICKLED FISH STEAKS

*Macchi Achar*

This dish is served cold and makes a lovely starter. It makes an ideal main course on a hot summer day served with a crisp salad. Make a day or two in advance to allow the flavours to blend.

SERVES 4–6

**Ingredients**
juice of 4 lemons
1 piece fresh ginger, 2.5cm/1 in long, finely sliced
2 cloves garlic, finely minced
2 fresh red chillies, finely chopped
3 green chillies, finely chopped

4 thick fish steaks (any firm fish)
4 tbsp vegetable oil
4–6 curry leaves
1 onion, finely chopped
½ tsp turmeric
1 tbsp coriander powder
150ml/¼ pint/½ cup pickling vinegar
3 tsp sugar

salt, to taste

1 In a bowl, mix the lemon juice with the ginger, garlic and chillies. Pat the fish dry with kitchen paper and rub the mixture on all sides of the fish. Allow to marinate for 3–4 hours in the refrigerator.

2 Heat the oil in a frying pan and fry the curry leaves, onion, turmeric and coriander until the onion is translucent.

3 Place the fish steaks in the frying pan with the marinade and cover with the onion mixture. After 5 minutes, turn the fish over gently to prevent damaging the steaks.

4 Pour in the vinegar and add the sugar and salt. Bring to the boil and then lower the heat and simmer until the fish is cooked. Delicately transfer the steaks to a large platter or individual serving dishes and pour over the vinegar mixture. Chill for 24 hours before serving.

# Prawns (Shrimp) Cooked with Okra

## *Jingha Aur Bhendi*

This dish has a sweet taste with a strong chilli flavour. It should be cooked fast to prevent the okra from breaking up and releasing its distinctive, sticky interior.

**SERVES 4–6**

**Ingredients**
4–6 tbsp oil
225g/8oz okra, washed, dried and left whole
4 cloves garlic, crushed

1 piece fresh ginger, 5cm/2in long, crushed
4–6 green chillies, cut diagonally
½ tsp turmeric
4–6 curry leaves
1 tsp cumin seeds
450g/1lb fresh king prawns (shrimp), peeled and

de-veined
salt, to taste
2 tsp brown sugar
juice of 2 lemons

**1** Heat the oil in a frying pan and fry the okra on a fairly high heat until they are slightly crisp and browned on all sides. Remove from the oil and keep aside on a piece of kitchen paper.

**2** In the same oil, gently fry the garlic, ginger, chillies, turmeric, curry leaves and cumin seeds for 2–3 minutes. Add the prawns (shrimp) and mix well. Cook until the prawns (shrimp) are tender.

**3** Add the salt, sugar, lemon juice and fried okra. Increase the heat and quickly fry for a further 5 minutes, stirring gently to prevent the okra from breaking. Adjust the seasoning, if necessary. Serve hot.

# Fried Whole Fish

## *Tali Huvey Macchi*

In southern India, fish is prepared daily in some form or other but most often it is just fried and served with a lentil curry and a nice hot pickle.

**SERVES 4–6**

**Ingredients**
1 small onion, coarsely chopped
4 cloves garlic, peeled
1 piece fresh ginger, 5cm/2in long, peeled
1 tsp turmeric
2 tsp chilli powder
salt, to taste
4 red mullets
vegetable oil, for shallow-frying
1 tsp cumin seeds
3 green chillies, finely sliced
lemon wedges, to serve

**1** Using a food processor, grind the first 6 ingredients to a smooth paste. Make gashes on both sides of the fish and rub them with the paste. Leave to rest for 1 hour. Lightly pat the fish dry with kitchen paper without removing the paste. Excess fluid will be released as the salt dissolves.

**2** Heat the oil in a large frying pan and fry the cumin seeds and chillies for about 1 minute. Add the fish and fry on one side without overlapping. When the first side is sealed, turn the fish over very gently to ensure they do not break. Fry until they are golden brown on both sides, drain well and serve hot with lemon or lime wedges.

# STUFFED FISH

*Bharey Huvey Macchi*

Every community in India prepares stuffed fish but the Parsi version must rank top of the list. The most popular fish in India is the pomfret. These are available from Indian and Chinese grocers or large supermarkets.

**SERVES 4**

**Ingredients**
2 large pomfrets, or Dover or lemon sole
2 tsp salt
juice of 1 lemon

**Masala**
8 tbsp desiccated (shredded) coconut
115g/4oz fresh coriander, including the tender
   stalks

8 green chillies (or to taste)
1 tsp cumin seeds
6 cloves garlic
2 tsp sugar
2 tsp lemon juice

### Cook's tip

In India, this fish dish is always steamed wrapped in banana leaves. Banana leaves are generally available from Indian or Chinese grocers but vine leaves from Greek food shops could be used instead.

1 Scale the fish and cut off the fins. Gut the fish and remove the heads, if desired. Using a sharp knife, make 2 diagonal gashes on each side, then pat dry with kitchen paper.

2 Rub the fish inside and out with salt and lemon juice and allow to stand for 1 hour. Pat dry thoroughly.

3 For the masala, grind all the ingredients together using a pestle and mortar or food processor, stuff the fish with the masala mixture and rub any remaining into the gashes and all over the fish on both sides.

4 Place each fish on a separate piece of greased foil. Tightly wrap the foil over each fish. Place in a steamer and steam for 20 minutes or bake for 30 minutes at 200°C/400°F/Gas Mark 6 or until cooked. Remove from the foil and serve hot.

# PARSI PRAWN (SHRIMP) CURRY

*Kalmino Patio*

This dish comes from the west coast of India, where fresh seafood is eaten in abundance. Fresh king prawns (shrimp) or 'tiger' prawns (shrimp) are ideal for Patio.

SERVES 4–6

**Ingredients**
4 tbsp vegetable oil
1 medium onion, finely sliced
6 cloves garlic, finely crushed
1 tsp chilli powder
1½ tsp turmeric
2 medium onions, finely chopped

50ml/2fl oz/¼ cup tamarind juice
1 tsp mint sauce
1 tbsp demerara sugar
salt, to taste
450g/1lb fresh king prawns (shrimp), peeled and
   de-veined
85g/3oz coriander leaves, chopped

1 Heat the oil in a frying pan and fry the sliced onion until golden brown. In a bowl, mix the garlic, chilli powder and turmeric with a little water to form a paste. Add to the browned onion and simmer for 3 minutes.

2 Add the chopped onions and fry until they become translucent, then fold in the tamarind juice, mint sauce, sugar and salt. Simmer for a further 3 minutes.

3 Pat the prawns (shrimp) dry with kitchen paper. Add to the spice mixture with a small amount of water and stir-fry until the prawns (shrimp) turn a bright orange/pink colour.

4 When the prawns (shrimp) are cooked, add the coriander leaves and stir-fry on a high heat for a few minutes to thicken the gravy. Serve hot.

# HOT AND SOUR MEAT AND LENTIL CURRY

*Dhansak*

This is one of the best-known Parsi dishes and is a favourite for Sunday lunch. This dish has a hot, sweet and sour flavour, through which should rise the slightly bitter flavour of fenugreek.

**SERVES 4–6**

**Ingredients**
6 tbsp vegetable oil
5 green chillies, chopped
1 piece fresh ginger, 2.5cm/1in long, crushed
3 cloves garlic, crushed
1 clove garlic, sliced
2 bay leaves
1 piece cinnamon stick, 5cm/2in long
900g/2lb lean lamb, cut in large pieces
575ml/1 pint/2½ cups water
175g/6oz red gram
50g/2oz each bengal gram, husked moong and red lentils
2 potatoes, cut and soaked in water
1 aubergine (egg plant), cut and soaked in water
4 onions, finely sliced, deep-fried and drained
50g/2oz fresh spinach, trimmed, washed and chopped or 50g/2oz frozen spinach, thawed and drained
25g/1oz fenugreek leaves, fresh or dried
115g/4oz carrots or pumpkin if in season
115g/4oz fresh coriander leaves, chopped
50g/2oz fresh mint leaves, chopped, or 1 tbsp mint sauce
2 tbsp dhansak masala
2 tbsp sambhar masala
salt, to taste
2 tsp brown sugar
4 tbsp tamarind juice

### Cook's tip

Chicken or prawns (shrimp) can be used instead of the lamb. If using chicken, reduce the cooking time so that the meat does not become shredded or stringy; if you are using prawns (shrimp), cook only until the tails turn bright orange/pink in colour.

1 Heat 3 tbsp of the oil in a saucepan or deep frying pan and fry the green chillies, ginger and crushed garlic cloves for 2 minutes. Add the bay leaves, cinnamon, lamb and water. Bring to the boil then simmer until the lamb is half cooked.

2 Drain the water into another pan and put the lamb aside. Add the lentils to the water and cook until they are tender. Mash the lentils with the back of a spoon.

3 Drain the aubergine (egg plant) and potatoes and add to the lentils with 3 of the deep-fried onions, the spinach, fenugreek and carrot or pumpkin. Add some hot water if the mixture is too thick. Cook until the vegetables are tender, then mash again with a spoon, keeping the vegetables a little coarse.

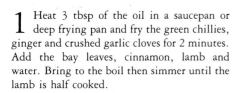

4 Heat 1 tbsp of the oil and gently fry the coriander and mint leaves (saving a little to garnish) with the dhansak and sambhar masala, salt and sugar. Add the lamb and fry gently for about 5 minutes.

5 Return the lamb and spices to the lentil and vegetable mixture and stir well. As lentils absorb fluids, adjust the consistency if necessary. Heat gently until the lamb is fully cooked.

6 Add the tamarind juice and mix well. Heat the remaining oil and fry the sliced clove of garlic until golden brown. Pour over the dhansak. Garnish with the remaining deep-fried onion and the reserved coriander and mint leaves. Serve hot.

# LENTILS SEASONED WITH FRIED SPICES

*Tarka Dhal*

Dhal is cooked in every house in India in one form or another. This recipe is a simplified version.

| SERVES 4–6 | 1 tsp turmeric | 1 clove garlic, crushed |
|---|---|---|
| | 1 large onion, sliced | 6 curry leaves |
| **Ingredients** | salt, to taste | 2 whole dried red chillies |
| 115g/4oz red gram, washed and picked over | 400g/14oz canned plum tomatoes, crushed | ¼ tsp asafoetida |
| 50g/2oz bengal gram, washed and picked over | 4 tbsp vegetable oil | deep-fried onions and fresh coriander leaves, to |
| 350ml/12fl oz/1½ cups water | ½ tsp mustard seeds | garnish |
| 4 whole green chillies | ½ tsp cumin seeds | |

1 Place the first 6 ingredients in a heavy pan and bring to the boil. Simmer, covered, until the lentils are soft and the water has evaporated.

2 Mash the lentils with the back of a spoon. When nearly smooth, add the salt and tomatoes and mix well. If necessary, thin the mixture with hot water.

3 Fry the remaining ingredients until the garlic browns. Pour the oil and spices over the lentils and cover. After 5 minutes, mix well, garnish and serve.

# SOUTH INDIAN LENTILS AND VEGETABLES

*Sambhar*

This is a favourite south Indian dish served for breakfast with dosai (Indian pancakes) or idli (rice dumplings).

| SERVES 4–6 | 6–8 curry leaves | zucchini, cauliflower, shallots and bell peppers) |
|---|---|---|
| | 2 cloves garlic, crushed | 4 tbsp tamarind juice |
| **Ingredients** | 2 tbsp desiccated (shredded) coconut | 4 firm tomatoes, quartered |
| 4 tbsp vegetable oil | 225g/8oz red lentils picked, washed and drained | 4 tbsp vegetable oil |
| ½ tsp mustard seeds | 2 tsp sambhar masala | 2 cloves garlic, finely sliced |
| ½ tsp cumin seeds | ½ tsp turmeric | a handful coriander leaves, chopped |
| 2 whole dried red chillies | 450ml/¾ pint/1½ cups water | |
| ¼ tsp asafoetida | 450g/1lb mixed vegetables (okra, courgettes/ | |

1 Fry the next 7 ingredients until the coconut browns. Mix in the lentils, sambhar masala, turmeric and water.

2 Simmer until the lentils are mushy. Add the vegetables, tamarind juice and tomatoes. Cook so the vegetables are crunchy.

3 Fry the garlic slices and coriander leaves. Pour over the lentils and vegetables. Mix at the table before serving.

# CURRIED CHICKPEAS WITH POTATO CAKES

## *Ragda Petis*

No other city in India is quite like Bombay. Its cuisine is typical of food you can buy right off the streets, which is the way the Bombayites like it – spicy, quick and nutritious.

MAKES 10–12

**Ingredients**
2 tbsp vegetable oil
2 tbsp coriander powder
2 tbsp cumin powder
½ tsp turmeric
½ tsp salt
½ tsp sugar
2 tbsp flour paste
450g/1lb boiled chickpeas (garbanzo beans),
drained
2 fresh green chillies, chopped
1 piece fresh ginger, 5cm/2in long, finely crushed
85g/3oz coriander leaves, chopped
2 firm tomatoes, chopped

**Petis**
450g/1lb potatoes, boiled and coarsely mashed
4 green chillies, finely chopped
50g/2oz coriander leaves, finely chopped
1½ tsp cumin powder
1 tsp amchur (dry mango powder)
salt, to taste
vegetable oil, for shallow-frying

1 For the Ragda, heat the oil in a saucepan and fry the coriander, cumin, turmeric, salt, sugar and flour paste until the water has evaporated and the oil separated.

2 Add the chickpeas (garbanzo beans), chillies, ginger, coriander leaves and tomatoes. Toss well and simmer for 5 minutes. Remove to a serving dish and keep warm.

3 To make the Petis, in a large mixing bowl mix the mashed potato with the green chillies, coriander, cumin and amchur powders and salt. Mix until all the ingredients are well blended.

4 Using your hands, shape the Petis mixture into little cakes. Heat the oil in a shallow frying pan or griddle and fry the cakes on both sides until golden brown. Transfer to a serving dish and serve with the Ragda.

# BLACK GRAM IN A SPICY CREAM SAUCE

*Masala Urad*

Dhabas – highway cafes – are very lively eating places serving a variety of dishes. This recipe is commonly served, and is one of the most popular.

### SERVES 4–6

**Ingredients**

175g/6oz black gram soaked overnight
50g/2oz red gram
100g/4fl oz/½ cup double (heavy) cream
100g/4fl oz/½ cup natural (plain) yoghurt
1 tsp cornflour (cornstarch)
3 tbsp ghee

1 onion, finely chopped
1 piece fresh ginger, 5cm/2in long, crushed
4 green chillies, chopped
1 tomato, chopped
½ tsp chilli powder
½ tsp turmeric
½ tsp cumin powder
salt, to taste
2 cloves garlic, sliced

1 Drain the black gram and place in a heavy pan with the red gram. Cover with water and bring to the boil. Reduce the heat, cover the pan and simmer until the gram are tender. The black gram will remain whole but the red gram will be mushy. Gently mash with a spoon. Allow to cool.

2 In a bowl, mix together the cream, yoghurt and cornflour (cornstarch). Mix the cream mixture into the gram without damaging the whole black gram grains.

3 Heat 1tbsp of the ghee in a frying pan and fry the onion, ginger, 2 of the green chillies and the tomato until the onion is soft. Add the spices and salt and fry for a further 2 minutes. Add it all to the gram mixture and mix well. Reheat and transfer to a heatproof serving dish and keep warm.

4 Heat the remaining ghee in a frying pan and fry the garlic slices and remaining chillies until the garlic slices are golden brown. Pour over the gram and serve, folding the garlic and chilli into the gram just before serving. Place extra cream on the table for the diners to add more if they wish.

# BLACK-EYED BEANS AND POTATO CURRY

### *Lobia Aloo*

Lobia are beige and kidney-shaped with a distinctive dark dot. This can be served as a starter or snack.

| SERVES 4–6 | 2 onions, finely chopped | 75ml/5 tbsp/⅓ cup tamarind juice |
|---|---|---|
| | 1 piece fresh ginger, 2.5cm/1in long, crushed | 2 potatoes, peeled, cubed and boiled |
| **Ingredients** | a few mint leaves | 115g/4oz coriander leaves, chopped |
| 225g/8oz lobia (black-eyed beans), soaked | 450ml/¾ pint/scant 2 cups water | 2 firm tomatoes, chopped |
| overnight and drained | 4 tbsp vegetable oil | salt, to taste |
| ¼ tsp bicarbonate of soda | ½ tsp each, turmeric, coriander, cumin and chilli | |
| 1 tsp five-spice powder | powders | |
| ¼ tsp asafoetida | 4 green chillies, chopped | |

1 Place the lobia with the next 7 ingredients in a heavy pan. Simmer until the beans are soft. Remove any excess water and reserve.

2 Gently fry the spice powders, chillies and tamarind juice, until they are well blended. Pour over the lobia and mix.

3 Add the potatoes, coriander leaves, tomatoes and salt. Mix well, and if necessary add a little reserved water. Reheat and serve.

# BENGAL GRAM AND BOTTLE GOURD CURRY

### *Doodhi Channa*

This is an Anglo-Indian version of dhal, which is characteristically hot, and with the dhals left whole.

| SERVES 4–6 | 1 onion, chopped | 450g/1lb bottle gourd or marrow, courgettes |
|---|---|---|
| | 2 cloves garlic, crushed | (zucchini), squash or pumpkin, peeled, pithed |
| **Ingredients** | 1 piece fresh ginger, 5cm/2in long, crushed | and sliced |
| 175g/6oz bengal gram, washed | 6–8 curry leaves | 4 tbsp tamarind juice |
| 450ml/¾ pint/scant 2 cups water | 1 tsp chilli powder | 2 tomatoes, chopped |
| 4 tbsp vegetable oil | 1 tsp turmeric | a handful fresh coriander leaves, chopped |
| 2 green chillies, chopped | salt, to taste | |

1 In a saucepan, cook the lentils in the water until the grains are tender but not mushy. Put aside without draining away any excess water.

2 Fry the chillies, onion, garlic, ginger, curry leaves, chilli powder and turmeric and salt. Add the gourd pieces and mix. Cover and cook until the gourd is soft.

3 Add the lentils and water and bring to the boil. Add the tamarind juice, tomatoes and coriander. Simmer until the gourd is cooked. Serve hot with a dry meat curry.

# FLAVOURED GREEN GRAM AND RICE

### *Kitchdee*

The whole spices are edible, but it is advisable to warn the diners about them.

| SERVES 4–6 | 1 piece ginger, 2.5cm/1 in long, shredded | salt, to taste |
|---|---|---|
| | 4 green chillies, chopped | 350g/12oz patna rice, washed and soaked for 20 |
| **Ingredients** | 4 whole cloves | minutes |
| 4 tbsp ghee | 1 piece cinnamon stick, 2.5cm/1 in long | 175g/6oz split green gram, washed and soaked for |
| 1 onion, finely chopped | 4 whole green cardamoms | 20 minutes |
| 2 cloves garlic, crushed | 1 tsp turmeric | 575ml/1 pint/2½ cups water |

1 Gently heat the ghee in a large heavy pan with a tight-fitting cover and fry the onion, garlic, ginger, chillies, cloves, cinnamon, cardamoms, turmeric and salt until the onion is soft and translucent.

2 Drain the rice and gram, add to the spices and sauté for 2–3 minutes. Add the water and bring to the boil. Reduce the heat, cover and cook for about 20–25 minutes or until all the water is absorbed.

3 Take the pan off the heat and leave to rest for 5 minutes. Just before serving gently toss the mixture with a flat spatula.

# DRY MOONG DHAL WITH COURGETTES (ZUCCHINI)

### *Sookhi Moong Aur Chingri*

Most dhal dishes are runny but this one provides texture with the addition of the courgettes (zucchini).

| SERVES 4–6 | 1 large onion, finely sliced | 6–8 curry leaves |
|---|---|---|
| | 2 cloves garlic, crushed | salt, to taste |
| **Ingredients** | 2 green chillies, chopped | ½ tsp sugar |
| 175g/6oz moong dhal | ½ tsp mustard seeds | 200g/7oz canned tomatoes, chopped |
| ½ tsp turmeric | ½ tsp cumin seeds | 225g/8oz courgettes (zucchini), cut into small |
| 300ml/½ pint/1¼ cups water | ¼ tsp asafoetida | pieces |
| 4 tbsp vegetable oil | a few coriander and mint leaves, chopped | 4 tbsp lemon juice |

1 In a saucepan, boil the moong dhal and turmeric in the water and then simmer until the dhal is cooked but not mushy. Drain and reserve both the liquid and the dhal.

2 Heat the oil in a frying pan and fry the remaining ingredients except the lemon juice. Cover and cook until the courgettes (zucchini) are nearly tender but still crunchy.

3 Fold in the drained dhal and the lemon juice. If the dish is too dry, add a small amount of the reserved water. Reheat and serve.

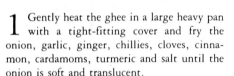

# BOMBAY POTATO

*Bumbai Aloo*

This authentic dish belongs to the Gujerati, a totally vegetarian sect and the largest population in Bombay.

SERVES 4–6

**Ingredients**
450g/1lb whole new potatoes
salt, to taste
1 tsp turmeric

4 tbsp vegetable oil
2 whole dried red chillies
6–8 curry leaves
2 onions, finely chopped
2 green chillies, finely chopped
50g/2oz coriander leaves, coarsely chopped

¼ tsp asafoetida
½ tsp each, cumin, mustard, onion, fennel and nigella seeds
lemon juice, to taste

1 Scrub the potatoes under running water and cut them into small pieces. Boil the potatoes in water with a little salt and ½ tsp of the turmeric until tender. Drain well then coarsely mash. Put aside.

2 Heat the oil and fry the red chillies and curry leaves until the chillies are nearly burnt. Add the onions, green chillies, coriander, remaining turmeric and spice seeds and cook until the onions are soft.

3 Fold in the potatoes and add a few drops of water. Cook on low heat for about 10 minutes, mixing well to ensure the even distribution of the spices. Add lemon juice to taste, and serve.

# CURRIED CAULIFLOWER

*Phul Gobi Salan*

In this dish the creamy, spiced coconut sauce disguises the strong smell of the spiced cauliflower.

SERVES 4–6

**Ingredients**
1 tbsp gram flour
100ml/4fl oz/½ cup water
1 tsp chilli powder

1 tbsp coriander powder
1 tsp cumin powder
1 tsp mustard powder
1 tsp turmeric
salt, to taste
4 tbsp vegetable oil

6–8 curry leaves
1 tsp cumin seeds
1 cauliflower, broken into florets
175ml/6fl oz/¾ cup thick coconut milk
juice of 2 lemons

1 Mix the gram flour with a little of the water to make a smooth paste. Add the chilli, coriander, cumin, mustard, turmeric and salt. Add the remaining water and keep mixing to blend all the ingredients well.

2 Heat the oil in a frying pan and fry the curry leaves and cumin seeds. Add the spice paste and simmer for about 5 minutes. If the gravy has become too thick, add a little hot water.

3 Add the cauliflower and coconut milk. Bring to the boil, reduce the heat, cover and cook until the cauliflower is tender but crunchy. Cook longer if you prefer. Add the lemon juice, mix well and serve hot.

# STUFFED OKRA

*Bharé Huvey Bhendi*

A delicious accompaniment to any dish, this can also be served on a bed of strained Greek yoghurt which gives an excellent contrast in flavour.

**SERVES 4–6**

**Ingredients**
225g/8oz large okra
1 tbsp amchur (dry mango powder)
½ tsp ginger powder
½ tsp cumin powder
½ tsp chilli powder (optional)
½ tsp turmeric
salt, to taste
a few drops of vegetable oil
2 tbsp cornflour (cornstarch), placed in a plastic bag
vegetable oil, for frying

1 Wash the okra and dry on kitchen paper. Carefully trim off the tops without making a hole. Using a sharp knife, make a slit lengthways in the centre of each okra but do not cut all the way through.

2 In a bowl, mix the amchur, ginger, cumin, chilli if using, turmeric and salt with a few drops of oil. Leave the mixture to rest for 1 or 2 hours.

3 Using your fingers, part the slit of each okra carefully without opening it all the way and fill each with as much filling as possible. Put all the okra into the plastic bag with the cornflour (cornstarch) and shake the bag carefully to cover the okra evenly.

4 Fill the frying pan with enough oil to sit 2.5cm/1in deep, heat it and fry the okra in small batches for about 5–8 minutes or until they are brown and slightly crisp. Serve hot.

# MIXED VEGETABLE CURRY

*Sabzi Salan*

This is a very delicately spiced vegetable dish that makes an appetizing snack when served with plain yoghurt. It is also a good accompaniment to a main meal of heavily spiced curries.

**SERVES 4–6**

**Ingredients**
350g/12oz mixed vegetables (beans, peas, potatoes, cauliflower, carrots, cabbage, mange-touts/snow peas and button mushrooms)
2 tbsp vegetable oil
1 tsp cumin seeds, freshly-roasted
½ tsp mustard seeds
½ tsp onion seeds
1 tsp turmeric
2 cloves garlic, crushed
6–8 curry leaves
1 whole dried red chilli
salt, to taste
1 tsp sugar
150ml/¼ pint/⅔ cup natural (plain) yoghurt mixed with 1 tsp cornflour (cornstarch)

1 Prepare all the vegetables you have chosen: string the beans, thaw the peas, if frozen; cube the potatoes; cut the cauliflower into florets; dice the carrots; shred the cabbage; top and tail the mange-touts (snow peas); wash the mushrooms and leave whole.

2 Heat a large pan with enough water to cook all the vegetables and bring to the boil. First add the potatoes and carrots and cook until nearly tender then add all the other vegetables and cook until still firm. All the vegetables should be crunchy except the potatoes. Drain well.

3 Heat the oil in a frying pan and fry the spices gently until the garlic is golden brown and the chilli nearly burnt. Reduce the heat.

4 Fold in the drained vegetables, add the sugar and salt and gradually add the yoghurt mixed with the cornflour (cornstarch). Heat to serving temperature and serve immediately.

# CURRIED SPINACH AND POTATO

*Palak Aloo Sag*

India is blessed with over 18 varieties of spinach. If you have access to an Indian or Chinese grocer, look out for some of the more unusual varieties.

SERVES 4–6

**Ingredients**
4 tbsp vegetable oil
225g/8oz potato
1 piece fresh ginger, 2.5cm/1in long, crushed
4 cloves garlic, crushed

1 onion, coarsely chopped
2 green chillies, chopped
2 whole dried red chillies, coarsely broken
1 tsp cumin seeds
salt, to taste
225g/8oz fresh spinach, trimmed, washed and chopped or 225g/8oz frozen spinach, thawed

and drained
2 firm tomatoes, coarsely chopped, to garnish

1 Wash the potatoes and cut into quarters. If using small new potatoes, leave them whole. Heat the oil in a frying pan and fry the potatoes until brown on all sides. Remove and put aside.

2 Remove the excess oil leaving 1 tbsp in the pan. Fry the ginger, garlic, onion, green chillies, dried chillies and cumin seeds until the onion is golden brown.

3 Add the potatoes and salt and stir well. Cook covered until the potatoes are tender when pierced with a sharp knife.

4 Add the spinach and stir well. Cook with the pan uncovered until the spinach is tender and all the excess fluids have evaporated. Garnish with the chopped tomatoes and serve hot.

# CURRIED MUSHROOMS, PEAS AND INDIAN CHEESE

## *Gucci Mattar Paneer*

Paneer is a traditional cheese made from rich milk and is most popular with northern Indians. Rajasthani farmers eat this dish for lunch with thick parathas as they work in the fields.

SERVES 4–6

**Ingredients**
6 tbsp ghee or vegetable oil
225g/8oz paneer, cubed
1 onion, finely chopped
a few mint leaves, chopped
50g/2oz coriander leaves, chopped
3 green chillies, chopped

3 cloves garlic
1 piece fresh ginger, 2.5cm/1in long, sliced
1 tsp turmeric
1 tsp chilli powder (optional)
1 tsp garam masala
salt, to taste
225g/8oz tiny button mushrooms, washed and left whole
225g/8oz frozen peas, thawed and drained

175ml/6fl oz/¾ cup natural (plain) yoghurt, mixed with 1 tsp cornflour (cornstarch)
tomatoes and coriander leaves, to garnish

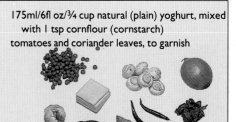

1 Heat the ghee or oil in a frying pan and fry the paneer cubes until they are golden brown on all sides. Remove and drain on kitchen paper.

2 Grind the onion, mint, coriander, chillies, garlic and ginger in a pestle and mortar or food processor to a fairly smooth paste. Remove and mix in the turmeric, chilli powder if using, garam masala and salt.

3 Remove excess ghee or oil from the pan leaving about 1 tbsp. Heat and fry the paste until the raw onion smell disappears and the oil separates.

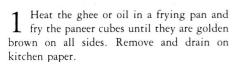

4 Add the mushrooms, peas and paneer. Mix well. Cool the mixture and gradually fold in the yoghurt. Simmer for about 10 minutes  Garnish with tomatoes and coriander and serve hot.

# CORN ON THE COB CURRY

*Butta Salan*

Corn-cobs are roasted on charcoal and rubbed with lemon juice, salt and chilli powder in India. In season, vendors fill the atmosphere with these delicious aromas. Corn is also a popular curry ingredient.

**SERVES 4–6**

**Ingredients**
4 whole corn-cobs, fresh, canned or frozen
vegetable oil, for frying
1 large onion, finely chopped
2 cloves garlic, crushed
1 piece fresh ginger, 5cm/2in long, crushed
½ tsp turmeric
½ tsp onion seeds
½ tsp cumin seeds
½ tsp five-spice powder
chilli powder, to taste
6–8 curry leaves
½ tsp sugar
200ml/7fl oz/scant 1 cup plain yoghurt

1 Cut each corn-cob in half, using a sharp, heavy knife or cleaver to make clean cuts and prevent damaging the kernels. Heat the oil in a wok and fry the corn pieces until golden brown on all sides. Remove the corn-cobs and keep aside.

2 Remove any excess oil leaving about 2 tbsp in the wok. Grind the onion, garlic and ginger to a paste using a pestle and mortar or food processor. Remove and mix in all the spices, curry leaves and sugar.

3 Heat the oil gently and fry the onion mixture until all the spices have blended well and the oil separates from the masala.

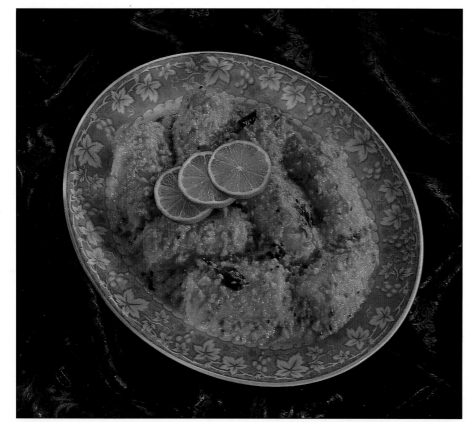

4 Cool the mixture and gradually fold in the yoghurt. Mix well until you have a smooth sauce. Add the corn to the mixture and mix well so all the pieces are evenly covered with the gravy. Gently reheat for about 10 minutes. Serve hot.

# CURRIED STUFFED (BELL) PEPPERS

*Bharey Huvey Mirchi Ka Salan*

This is one of the most famous dishes of Deccan. Hot, spicy and extremely delicious, it is often prepared for weddings. It is made with extra oil several days in advance to allow the spices to mature.

SERVES 4–6

**Ingredients**
1 tbsp sesame seeds
1 tbsp white poppy seeds
1 tsp coriander seeds
4 tbsp desiccated (shredded) coconut
½ onion, sliced
1 piece fresh ginger, 2.5cm/1 in long, sliced

4 cloves garlic, sliced
a handful of coriander leaves
2 green chillies
4 tbsp vegetable oil
2 potatoes, boiled and coarsely mashed
salt, to taste
2 each, green, red and yellow (bell) peppers
2 tbsp sesame oil
1 tsp cumin seeds

4 green chillies, slit
4 tbsp tamarind juice

**1** In a frying pan, dry-fry the sesame, poppy and coriander seeds, then add the desiccated (shredded) coconut and continue to roast until the coconut turns golden brown. Add the onion, ginger, garlic, coriander, and chillies and roast for a further 5 minutes. Cool, and grind to a paste using a pestle and mortar or food processor. Put aside.

**2** Heat 2 tbsp of the vegetable oil in a frying pan and fry the ground paste for 4–5 minutes. Add the potatoes and salt and stir well until the spices have blended evenly into the potatoes.

**3** Slice the tail ends off the (bell) peppers and reserve. Remove the seeds and any white pith. Fill the (bell) peppers with even amounts of the potato mixture and replace the tail ends on the top.

**4** Heat the sesame oil and remaining vegetable oil in a frying pan and fry the cumin seeds and the green chillies. When the chillies turn white, add the tamarind juice and bring to the boil. Place the (bell) peppers over the mixture, cover the pan and cook until the peppers are nearly done.

# POTATOES IN A HOT RED SAUCE

*Lal Batata*

This dish should be hot and sour but, if you wish, reduce the chillies and add extra tomato purée (paste) instead.

| SERVES 4–6 | 1 ½ tsp cumin seeds | salt, to taste |
| --- | --- | --- |
| **Ingredients** | 4 cloves garlic | 1 tsp sugar |
| 450g/1lb small new potatoes, washed and dried | 6 tbsp vegetable oil | ¼ tsp asafoetida |
| 25g/1oz whole dried red chillies, preferably | 4 tbsp thick tamarind juice | coriander leaves and lemon wedges, to garnish |
| kashmiri | 2 tbsp tomato purée (paste) | |
| | 4 curry leaves | |

**1** Boil the potatoes until they are fully cooked, ensuring they do not break. To test, insert a thin sharp knife into the potatoes. It should come out clean when the potatoes are fully cooked. Drain well.

**2** Soak the chillies for 5 minutes in warm water. Drain and grind with the cumin seeds and garlic to a coarse paste using a pestle and mortar or food processor.

**3** Fry the paste, tamarind juice, tomato purée (paste), curry leaves, salt, sugar and asafoetida until the oil separates. Add the potatoes. Reduce the heat, cover and simmer for 5 minutes. Garnish and serve.

# CUCUMBER CURRY

*Kakri Ka Salan*

This makes a pleasant accompaniment to fish dishes and may be served cold with cooked meats.

| SERVES 4–6 | salt, to taste | 2 dried red chillies |
| --- | --- | --- |
| | 1 tsp sugar | 1 tsp cumin seeds |
| **Ingredients** | 1 large cucumber, cut into small pieces | 1 tsp mustard seeds |
| 100ml/4fl oz/½ cup water | 1 large red (bell) pepper, cut into small pieces | 4–6 curry leaves |
| 115g/4oz creamed coconut | 50g/2oz salted peanuts, coarsely crushed | 4 cloves garlic, crushed |
| ½ tsp turmeric | 4 tbsp vegetable oil | a few whole salted peanuts, to garnish |

**1** Bring the water to the boil in a heavy pan and add the creamed coconut, turmeric, salt and sugar. Simmer until the coconut dissolves to obtain a smooth, thick sauce.

**2** Add the cucumber, red (bell) pepper and crushed peanuts and simmer for about 5 minutes. Transfer to a heat-proof serving dish and keep warm.

**3** Fry the chillies and cumin with the mustard seeds until they start to pop. Reduce the heat, add the curry leaves and garlic and fry. Pour over the cucumber mixture and stir well. Garnish and serve hot.

# HOT LIME PICKLE

*Nimbu Achar*

A good lime pickle is not only delicious served with any meal, but it increases the appetite and aids digestion.

| MAKES 450G/1LB/2 CUPS | 225g/8oz salt | 15g/½oz turmeric |
| --- | --- | --- |
| | 50g/2oz fenugreek powder | 575ml/1pint/2½ cups mustard oil |
| **Ingredients** | 50g/2oz mustard powder | 1 tsp asafoetida |
| 25 limes | 150g/5oz chilli powder | 25g/1oz yellow mustard seeds, crushed |

1 Cut each lime into 8 pieces and remove the pips, if you wish. Place the limes in a large sterilized jar or glass bowl. Add the salt and toss with the limes. Cover and leave in a warm place until they become soft and dull brown in colour, for 1 to 2 weeks.

2 Mix together the fenugreek, mustard powder, chilli powder and turmeric and add to the limes. Cover and leave to rest in a warm place for a further 2 or 3 days.

3 Heat the mustard oil in a frying pan and fry the asafoetida and mustard seeds. When the oil reaches smoking point, pour it over the limes. Mix well, cover with a clean cloth and leave in a warm place for about 1 week before serving.

# GREEN CHILLI PICKLE

*Mirchi Ka Achar*

Southern India is the source of some of the hottest curries and pickles, which are said to cool the body.

| MAKES 450–550G/1–1¼ LB/2–2½ CUPS | 25g/1oz turmeric | 150ml/¼ pint/⅔ cup mustard oil |
| --- | --- | --- |
| | 50g/2oz garlic cloves | 20 small garlic cloves, peeled and left whole |
| **Ingredients** | 150ml/¼ pint/⅔ cup white vinegar | 450g/1lb small green chillies, washed, dried and |
| 50g/2oz yellow mustard seeds, crushed | 85g/3oz sugar | halved |
| 50g/2oz freshly-ground cumin seeds | 2 tsp salt | |

1 Mix the mustard seeds, cumin, turmeric, crushed garlic, vinegar, sugar and salt together in a sterilized glass bowl. Cover with a cloth and allow to rest for 24 hours. This enables the spices to infuse and the sugar and salt to melt.

2 Heat the mustard oil and gently fry the spice mixture for about 5 minutes. (Keep a window open while cooking with mustard oil as it is pungent and the smoke may irritate the eyes.) Add the garlic cloves and fry for a further 5 minutes.

3 Add the chillies and cook gently until tender but still green in colour. This will take about 30 minutes on a low heat. Cool thoroughly and pour into sterilized bottles, ensuring the oil is evenly distributed if you are using more than one bottle. Leave to rest for a week before serving.

# SPICED YOGHURT

*Tarka Dahi*

Yoghurt is always a welcome accompaniment to hot curries. This has been given a final fry with spices just to flavour the yoghurt slightly.

MAKES 450ML/¾ PINT/2 CUPS

**Ingredients**
450ml/¾ pint/scant 2 cups plain yoghurt
½ tsp freshly-ground fennel seeds
salt, to taste
½ tsp sugar
4 tbsp vegetable oil
1 whole dried red chilli
¼ tsp mustard seeds
¼ tsp cumin seeds
4–6 curry leaves
a pinch each, asafoetida and turmeric

1 In a heat-proof serving dish, mix together the yoghurt, fennel seeds, salt and sugar and chill until you are nearly ready to serve.

2 Heat the oil in a frying pan and fry the chilli, mustard and cumin seeds, curry leaves, asafoetida and turmeric. When the chilli turns dark, pour the oil and spices over the yoghurt. Fold the yoghurt together with the spices at the table before serving.

# YOGHURT SALAD

*Mava Raitha*

Raithas are served to cool the effect of hot curries. Cucumber and mint raitha is most commonly served, so why not try a variation?

SERVES 4

**Ingredients**
350ml/12fl oz/1½ cups natural (plain) yoghurt
85g/3oz seedless grapes, washed and dried
50g/2oz shelled walnuts
2 firm bananas
1 tsp sugar
salt, to taste
1 tsp freshly-ground cumin seeds
¼ tsp freshly-roasted cumin seeds, chilli powder or paprika, to garnish

1 Place the yoghurt in a chilled bowl and add the grapes and walnuts. Slice the bananas directly into the bowl and fold in gently before the bananas turn brown.

2 Add the sugar, salt and ground cumin, and gently mix together. Chill, and just before serving, sprinkle on the cumin seeds, chilli powder or paprika.

# TOMATO SALAD

*Tamatar Kasondi*

This is a simple salad served with most meals. It provides a contrast to hot curries, with its crunchy texture and refreshing ingredients.

SERVES 4–6

**Ingredients**
2 limes
½ tsp sugar
salt and freshly-ground black pepper, to taste
2 onions, finely chopped
4 firm tomatoes, finely chopped
½ cucumber, finely chopped
1 green chilli, finely chopped
a few coriander leaves, chopped
a few mint leaves, to garnish

1 Extract the juice of the limes into a small bowl and add the sugar, salt and pepper. Allow to rest until the sugar and salt have dissolved. Mix together well.

2 Add the onions, tomatoes, cucumber, chilli and coriander leaves, reserving a few. Chill, and garnish with coriander and mint before serving.

# FRESH CORIANDER RELISH

## *Hara Dhaniya Chutney*

Delicious as an accompaniment to kebabs, samosas and bhajias, this relish can also be used as a spread for cucumber or tomato sandwiches.

MAKES 400G/14OZ/1¾ CUPS

**Ingredients**
2 tbsp vegetable oil
1 dried red chilli
¼ tsp each, cumin, fennel and onion seeds
¼ tsp asafoetida
4 curry leaves
115g/4oz desiccated (shredded) coconut
2 tsp sugar
salt, to taste
3 green chillies
175g–225g/6–8oz coriander leaves
4 tbsp mint sauce
juice of 3 lemons

1 Fry the red chilli, cumin, fennel and onion seeds, asafoetida, curry leaves, desiccated (shredded) coconut, sugar and salt until the coconut turns golden brown. Cool.

2 Grind the spice mixture with the green chillies, coriander leaves and mint sauce. Moisten with lemon juice. Remove, and chill before serving.

# TOMATO CHUTNEY

## *Kachoomber*

This delicious relish is especially suited to lentil dishes. If kept refrigerated, it can be made a week before serving.

MAKES 450–500G/16–18OZ/2–2¼ CUPS

**Ingredients**
6 tbsp vegetable oil
1 piece cinnamon stick, 5cm/2in long
4 cloves
1 tsp freshly-roasted cumin seeds
1 tsp nigella seeds
4 bay leaves
1 tsp mustard seeds, crushed
4 cloves garlic, crushed
1 piece fresh ginger, 5cm/2in long, crushed
1 tsp chilli powder
1 tsp turmeric
4 tbsp brown sugar
800g/1¾ lb canned, chopped tomatoes, drained (reserving juices)

1 Heat the oil on a medium heat and fry the cinnamon, cloves, cumin and nigella seeds, bay leaves and mustard seeds for about 5 minutes. Add the garlic and fry until golden.

2 Add the ginger, chilli powder, turmeric, sugar and the reserved tomato juices. Simmer until reduced, add the tomatoes and cook for 15–20 minutes. Cool and serve.

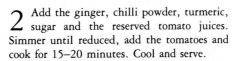

# MANGO CHUTNEY

## *Kairi Ki Chutni*

Chutneys are usually served as an accompaniment to curry but this one is particularly nice served in a cheese sandwich or as a dip with papadums.

MAKES 450G/1LB/2 CUPS

**Ingredients**
50ml/2fl oz/¼ cup malt vinegar
½ tsp dried chillies, crushed
6 whole cloves
6 whole peppercorns
1 tsp roasted cumin seeds
½ tsp onion seeds
salt, to taste
175g/6oz sugar
450g/1lb unripe mango, peeled and cubed
1 piece fresh ginger, 5cm/2in long, finely sliced
2 cloves garlic, crushed
thin peel of 1 orange or lemon (optional)

1 In a saucepan, heat the vinegar with the chillies, cloves, peppercorns, cumin and onion seeds, salt and sugar. Simmer until the flavours of the spices infuse into the vinegar – about 15 minutes on low heat.

2 Add the mango, ginger, garlic and peel, if using. Simmer until the mango is mushy and most of the vinegar has evaporated. When cool, pour into sterilized bottles. Leave for a few days before serving.

# HOT TOMATO SAMBAL

## *Sambal Tomat*

Sambals are placed on the table as a condiment and are used mainly for dipping meat and fish. They are quite strong and should be used sparingly.

MAKES 120ML/4 FL OZ/½ CUP

**Ingredients**
3 ripe tomatoes
½ tsp salt
1 tsp chilli sauce
4 tbsp fish sauce, or soy sauce
1 tbsp chopped coriander leaves

1 Cover the tomatoes with boiling water to loosen the skins. Remove the skins, halve, discard the seeds and chop finely.

2 Place the chopped tomatoes in a bowl, add the salt, chilli sauce, fish sauce or soy sauce, and coriander.

# HOT CHILLI AND GARLIC DIPPING SAUCE

## *Sambal Kecap*

This sambal is particularly strong, so warn guests who are unaccustomed to spicy foods.

MAKES 120ML/4FL OZ/½ CUP

**Ingredients**
1 clove garlic, crushed
2 small red chillies, seeded and finely chopped
2 tsp sugar
1 tsp tamarind sauce
4 tbsp soy sauce
juice of ½ lime

1 Pound the garlic, chillies and sugar until smooth using a pestle and mortar, or grind in a food processor.

2 Add the tamarind sauce, soy sauce and lime juice.

# CUCUMBER SAMBAL

## *Sambal Selamat*

This sambal has a piquant flavour without the hotness of chillies found in other recipes.

MAKES 150ML/5FL OZ/⅔ CUP

**Ingredients**
1 clove garlic, crushed
1 tsp fennel seeds
2 tsp sugar
½ tsp salt
2 shallots, or 1 small onion, finely sliced
100ml/4fl oz/½ cup rice or white wine vinegar
¼ cucumber, finely diced

1 Place the garlic, fennel seeds, sugar and salt in a pestle and mortar and pound finely. Alternatively, grind the ingredients thoroughly in a food processor.

2 Stir in the shallots or onion, vinegar and cucumber and allow to stand for at least 6 hours to allow the flavours to combine.

# EXOTIC FRUIT SALAD

*Hoa Qua Tron*

A variety of fruits can be used for this salad depending on what is available. Look out for mandarin oranges, star fruit, paw paw, Cape gooseberries and passion fruit.

| SERVES 4–6 | 1 medium pineapple |
| --- | --- |
| | 1 mango, peeled and sliced |
| **Ingredients** | 2 bananas, sliced |
| 85g/3oz/6tbsp sugar | 8 lychees, fresh or canned |
| 300ml/½ pint/1¼ cups water | 225g/8oz fresh strawberries, trimmed and halved |
| 2 tbsp stem ginger syrup | 2 pieces stem ginger, cut into sticks |
| 2 pieces star anise | |
| 1 piece cinnamon stick, 2.5cm/1in long | |
| 1 clove | |
| juice of ½ lemon | |
| 2 sprigs mint | |

1 Measure the sugar into a saucepan, and add the water, ginger syrup, spices, lemon juice and mint. Bring to the boil and simmer for 3 minutes. Strain into a large bowl and allow to cool.

2 Remove both the top and bottom from the mango and remove the outer skin. Stand the mango on one end and remove the flesh in two pieces either side of the flat stone (pit). Slice evenly and add to the syrup. Add the bananas, lychees, strawberries and ginger. Chill until ready to serve.

3 Cut the pineapple in half down the centre. Loosen the flesh with a small serrated knife and remove to form two boat shapes. Cut the flesh into large chunks and place in the cooled syrup.

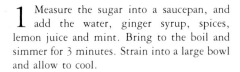

4 Spoon the fruit salad into the pineapple halves and bring to the table on a large serving dish. There will be enough fruit salad left over to refill the pineapple halves.

# AVOCADO SALAD

*Makhan Chaat*

In India, avocados are called butter fruit, reflecting their subtle taste. This delicate dish makes a good starter.

SERVES 4

**Ingredients**
2 avocados
75ml/5 tbsp/⅓ cup natural (plain) yoghurt, beaten

115g/4oz cottage cheese with chives
I clove garlic, crushed
2 green chillies, finely chopped
salt and pepper, to taste
a little lemon juice

a few lettuce leaves, shredded (a mixed variety makes a good display)
paprika and mint leaves, to garnish

1 Halve the avocados and remove the stones (pits). Gently scoop out the flesh, reserving the skins, and cut into small cubes. In a bowl, mix the yoghurt, cottage cheese, garlic, chillies and salt and pepper and fold in the avocado cubes. Chill in the refrigerator.

2 Rub the avocado skins with some lemon juice and line each cavity with some shredded lettuce. Top with the chilled mixture, garnish with the paprika and mint leaves and serve immediately.

# INDIAN FRUIT SALAD

*Phul Chaat*

This is a very appetizing and refreshing salad, with a typically Indian combination of citrus fruits seasoned with salt and pepper. It will provide the perfect ending to a heavy meal.

SERVES 6

**Ingredients**
115g/4oz seedless green and black grapes
225g/8oz canned mandarin segments, drained

2 navel oranges, peeled and segmented
225g/8oz canned grapefruit segments, drained
balls from one honeydew melon
balls from ½ watermelon (when in season)
I fresh mango, peeled and sliced

juice of I lemon
salt and freshly-ground black pepper, to taste
½ tsp sugar
¼ tsp freshly-ground cumin seeds

1 Place all the fruit in a large serving bowl and add the lemon juice. Gently toss to prevent damaging the fruit.

2 Mix together the remaining ingredients and sprinkle over the fruit. Gently toss, chill thoroughly and serve.

# RICE PUDDING

*Kheer*

Both Muslim and Hindu communities prepare this sweet, which is traditionally served at mosques and temples.

| SERVES 4–6 | 1 piece cinnamon stick, 5cm/2in long | 1 tsp ground cardamom |
|---|---|---|
| | 175g/6oz soft brown sugar | 50g/2oz sultanas (white raisins) |
| **Ingredients** | 115g/4oz coarsely-ground rice | 25g/1oz almond flakes |
| 1 tbsp ghee | 1.1l/2 pints/5 cups full cream (whole) milk | ½ tsp freshly-ground nutmeg, to serve |

1 In a heavy pan, melt the ghee and fry the cinnamon and sugar. Keep frying until the sugar begins to caramelize. Reduce the heat immediately when this happens.

2 Add the rice and half the milk. Bring to the boil, stirring constantly to avoid the milk boiling over. Reduce the heat and simmer until the rice is cooked, stirring regularly.

3 Add the remaining milk, cardamom, sultanas (white raisins) and almonds and leave to simmer, but keep stirring to prevent the kheer from sticking to the base of the pan. When the mixture has thickened, serve hot or cold, sprinkled with the nutmeg.

# VERMICELLI PUDDING

*Shirkhuma*

This sweet is prepared by Muslims very early in the morning of Id-ul-Fitr, the feast after the 30 days of Ramadan.

| SERVES 4–6 | 25g/1oz almond flakes | 1.1l/2 pints/4 cups full cream (whole) milk |
|---|---|---|
| | 25g/1oz pistachios, slivered | 4 tbsp dark brown sugar |
| **Ingredients** | 25g/1oz cudapah nuts | 1 sachet saffron powder |
| 6 tbsp ghee | 50g/2oz sultanas (white raisins) | |
| 115g/4oz vermicelli, coarsely broken | 50g/2oz dates, stoned (pitted) and slivered | |

1 Heat 4 tbsp of the ghee in a frying pan and sauté the vermicelli until golden brown. (If you are using the Italian variety, sauté it a little longer.) Remove and keep aside.

2 Heat the remaining ghee and fry the nuts, sultanas (white raisins) and dates until the sultanas (white raisins) swell. Add to the vermicelli.

3 Heat the milk in a large heavy pan and add the sugar. Bring to the boil, add the vermicelli mixture and boil, stirring constantly. Reduce the heat and simmer until the vermicelli is soft and you have a fairly thick pudding. Fold in the saffron powder and serve hot or cold.

# Indian Ice Cream

*Kulfi*

Kulfi-wallahs (ice cream vendors) have always made kulfi, and continue to this day, without using modern freezers. Kulfi is packed into metal cones sealed with dough and then churned in clay pots until set. Try this method – it works extremely well in an ordinary freezer.

**SERVES 4–6**

**Ingredients**
3 × 400ml/14fl oz cans evaporated milk
3 egg whites, whisked until peaks form
350g/12oz icing (confectioners') sugar
1 tsp cardamom powder
1 tbsp rose water
175g/6oz pistachios, chopped
85g/3oz sultanas (white raisins)
85g/3oz sliced almonds
25g/1oz glacé (candied) cherries, halved

1 Remove the labels from the cans of evaporated milk and lay the cans down into a pan with a tight-fitting cover. Fill the pan with water to reach three-quarters up the cans. Bring to the boil, cover and simmer for 20 minutes. When cool, remove and chill the cans in the refrigerator for 24 hours.

2 Open the cans and empty the milk into a large, chilled bowl. Whisk until it doubles in quantity, then fold in the whisked egg whites and icing (confectioners') sugar.

3 Gently fold in the remaining ingredients, seal the bowl with cling film (plastic wrap) and leave in the freezer for 1 hour.

4 Remove the ice cream from the freezer and mix well with a fork. Transfer to a serving container and return to the freezer for a final setting. Remove from the freezer 10 minutes before serving.

# ALMOND CURD JUNKET

*Xing Ren Tou Fou*

Also known as Almond Float, this is usually made from agar-agar or isinglass, though gelatine can also be used.

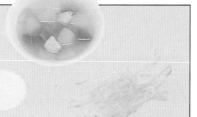

**SERVES 4–6**

**Ingredients**

7g/¼oz agar-agar or isinglass or 25g/1oz
    gelatine powder
about 575ml/1 pint/2½ cups water
4 tbsp granulated or caster (superfine) sugar

300ml/½ pint/1¼ cups milk
1 tsp almond essence (extract)
fresh or canned mixed fruit salad with syrup, to
    serve

1 In a saucepan, dissolve the agar-agar or isinglass in about half of the water over a gentle heat. This will take at least 10 minutes. If using gelatine, follow the instructions.

2 In a separate saucepan, dissolve the sugar in the remaining water over a medium heat. Add the milk and the almond essence (extract), blending well, but do not boil.

3 Mix the milk and sugar with the agar-agar or isinglass mixture in a large serving bowl. When cool, place in the refrigerator for 2–3 hours to set.

4 To serve, cut the 'junket' into small cubes and spoon into a serving dish or into individual bowls. Pour the fruit salad, with the syrup, over the junket and serve.

# TOFFEE APPLES

*Ba Tsu Ping Guo*

A variety of fruits, such as banana and pineapple, can be prepared and cooked the same way.

**SERVES 4**

**Ingredients**
4 firm eating apples, peeled and cored
115g/4oz/1 cup plain (all-purpose) flour
about 100ml/4fl oz/½ cup cold water
1 egg, beaten

vegetable oil, for deep-frying, plus 2 tbsp for the toffee
115g/4oz/½ cup granulated or caster (superfine) sugar

1 Cut each apple into 8 pieces. Dust each piece with a little of the flour.

2 Sift the remaining flour into a mixing bowl, then slowly add the cold water and stir to make a smooth batter. Add the beaten egg and blend well.

3 Heat the oil in a wok. Dip the apple pieces in the batter and deep-fry for about 3 minutes or until golden. Remove and drain.

4 Heat 2 tbsp of the oil in the wok, add the sugar and stir continuously until the sugar has caramelized. Quickly add the apple pieces and blend well so that each piece of apple is coated with the 'toffee'. Dip the apple pieces in cold water to harden before serving.

# MANGO SORBET (SHERBET) WITH SAUCE

*Baraf Ke Aamb*

After a heavy meal, this makes a very refreshing dessert. Mango is said to be one of the oldest fruits cultivated in India, having been brought by Lord Shiva for his beautiful wife, Parvathi.

| SERVES 4–6 | peel of 1 orange and 1 lemon, grated |
| --- | --- |
| | 4 egg whites, whisked until peaks form |
| **Ingredients** | 50g/2oz caster (superfine) sugar |
| 900g/2lb mango pulp | 100ml/4fl oz/½ cup double (heavy) cream |
| ½ tsp lemon juice | 50g/2oz icing (confectioners') sugar |

1 In a large, chilled bowl, mix 425g/15oz of the mango pulp with the lemon juice and the peel.

2 Gently fold in the egg whites and caster (superfine) sugar. Cover with cling film (plastic wrap) and place in the freezer for at least 1 hour.

3 Remove and beat again. Transfer to an ice cream container, and freeze until fully set.

4 Whip the double (heavy) cream with the icing (confectioners') sugar and the remaining mango pulp. Chill the sauce for 24 hours. Remove the sorbet (sherbet) 10 minutes before serving. Scoop out individual servings and cover with a generous helping of mango sauce. Serve immediately.

# TEA AND FRUIT PUNCH

### *Chai Sherbet*

This delicious punch may be served hot or cold. White wine or brandy may be added to taste.

| MAKES 875ML/1¾ PINTS/3½ CUPS | 4 cloves | 1 lemon, sliced |
|---|---|---|
| | 2½ tsp Earl Grey tea leaves | 1 small orange, sliced |
| **Ingredients** | 175g/6oz sugar | ½ cucumber, sliced |
| 575ml/1pint/2½ cups water | 450ml/¾ pint/1½ cups tropical soft drink | |
| 1 cinnamon stick | concentrate | |

1 Bring the water to the boil in a saucepan with the cinnamon and cloves. Remove from the heat and add the tea leaves and allow to brew for 5 minutes. Stir and strain into a large chilled bowl.

2 Add the sugar and the soft drink concentrate and allow to rest until the sugar has dissolved and the mixture cooled. Place the fruit and cucumber in a chilled punch bowl and pour over the tea mix. Chill for 24 hours before serving.

# BUTTERMILK

### *Lassi*

Buttermilk is prepared by churning yoghurt with water and then removing the fat. To make this refreshing drink without churning, use low-fat natural (plain) yoghurt.

| SERVES 4 | 300ml/½ pint/1¼ cups water | salt and freshly-ground black pepper, to taste |
|---|---|---|
| | 1 piece fresh ginger, 2.5cm/1in long, finely crushed | a few coriander leaves, chopped, to garnish |
| **Ingredients** | 2 green chillies, finely chopped | |
| 450ml/¾ pint/1½ cups natural (plain) yoghurt | ½ tsp cumin powder | |

1 In a bowl, whisk the yoghurt and water until well blended. The consistency should be that of full cream (whole) milk. Adjust by adding more water if necessary.

2 Add the ginger, chillies and cumin powder, season with the salt and pepper and mix well. Divide into 4 serving glasses and chill. Garnish with coriander before serving.

### Cook's tip

To make sweet lassi, mix the yoghurt and water together with 6 tbsp sugar, 1 tsp freshly-ground cumin powder, ½ tsp cardamom powder and a pinch of salt and pepper. Whisk all the ingredients together, chill and serve.

# COCONUT MILK

Coconut milk is used to enrich and flavour many dishes in the Far East. Only the Japanese choose not to include it in their cooking. Coconut milk is not, as many suppose, the liquid found inside the nut. Although this thin liquid does make a refreshing drink, the coconut milk used for cooking is processed from the white flesh of the nut. If left to stand, the thick part of the milk will rise to the surface like cream. If the milk is cold the thick part of the milk will separate more easily. Choose a coconut with plenty of milk inside. Shake the nut firmly. If you cannot hear the milk sloshing around, the flesh will be difficult to remove. If you can find a coconut with its green husk and fibre attached, the flesh will almost certainly be soft and creamy white. Fresh coconut milk will keep in a cool place for up to 10 days. If kept in the refrigerator, allow to soften at room temperature before using.

MAKES 400ml/14fl oz/1¾ cups

**Ingredients**
2 fresh coconuts
1.1 litres/2 pints/5 cups water, off the boil

1 Hold the coconut over a bowl to collect the liquid. With the back of a large knife or cleaver, crack open the coconut by striking it cleanly.

2 Scrape out the white meat with a citrus zester or a rounded butter curler. Place the coconut meat in a food processor with half of the water.

3 Process for 1 minute, then pass through a food mill or mouli fitted with a fine disk, catching the milk in a bowl beneath. Alternatively, squeeze the coconut meat with your hands and press through a nylon strainer. Return the coconut meat to the food processor or mill with the remainder of the water, blend and press for a second time. Allow the milk to settle for 30 minutes (creamy solids will rise to the surface). Sometimes the solids should be poured off and added later as a thickener.

### Cook's tip

Coconut milk can be obtained directly from coconut flesh – this gives the creamiest milk; from a can – which may be expensive; as a soluble powder and as creamed coconut which is sold in block form. Powder and creamed coconut make a poor milk, but are useful additions to sauces and dressings.

# STOCKISTS AND SUPPLIERS

## United Kingdom
### Indian food and equipment

**M. and S. Patel** 372–382 Romford Road, London E7 8BS
(081) 472-6201

**Rafi's Spice Box** c/o 31 Schoolfield, Glemsford, Suffolk, CO10 7RE (mail order)

**The Spice Shop** 115–117 Drummond Street, London NW1 2HL
(071) 387-4526

## United States
### Indian food and equipment

#### Arizona
**G&L Import-Export Corp.** 4828 East 22nd Street, Tuscon, Arizona, 85706, (602) 790-9016

**Manila Oriental Foodmart** 3557 West Dunlap Avenue, Phoenix, Arizona, 85021, (602) 841-2977

#### California
**Indian Food Mill** 650 San Bruno Avenue East, San Bruno, California, 94014, (415) 583-6559

#### Connecticut
**India Spice & Gift Shop** 3295 Fairfield Avenue, Fairfield, Connecticut, 06605, (203) 384-0666

#### Florida
**Grocery Mahat & Asian Spices** 1026 South Military Trail, West Palm Beach, Florida, 33436, (407) 433-3936

#### Illinois
**Indian Groceries & Spices** 7300 St Louis Avenue, Skokie, Illinois 60076, (708) 2480

#### Maryland
**India Supermarket** 8107 Fenton Street, Silver Springs, Maryland, 20910, (301) 589-8423

#### Massachusetts
**India Groceries** Oak Square, Boston, Massachusetts, 02111, (617) 254-5540

#### New Jersey
**Maharaja Indian Foods** 130 Speedwell Avenue, Morristown, New Jersey, 07960, (210) 829-0048

#### New York
**Indian Groceries and Spices** 61 Wythe Avenue, Brooklyn, New York, 11211, (718) 963-0477

#### Ohio
**Crestview Market** 200 Crestview Road, Columbus, Ohio, 43202 (614) 267-2723

#### Pennsylvania
**Gourmail Inc.** Drawer 516, Berwyn, Pennsylvania, 19312 (215) 296-4620

#### Texas
**MGM Indian Foods** 9200 Lamar Boulevard, Austin, Texas, 78513, (512) 835-6937

# INDEX

Almonds
    Almond curd junket, 87
    flakes, 9
*Andoan ka salan*, 42
Aniseed, 8
Apples, toffee, 90
Apricots, 9
Asafoetida, 9
Aubergine, 9
Avocado salad, 82

*Ba Tsu Ping guo*, 88
*Baraf ke aamb*, 89
Basmati rice, 9
Bay leaves, 9
Beef
    curried mince, 34
    hot dry meat curry, 30
    Madras, 36
    potato cakes with stuffing, 13
    spicy kebabs, 32
    spicy meat loaf, 32
    steak and kidney with spinach, 35
Bengal gram, 9
    Bengal gram and bottle gourd curry, 62
Bhajias, 10
*Bharey huvey macchi*, 54
*Bharey huvey mirchi ka salan*, 73
*Bharé huvey bhendi*, 68
Black cumin, 8
Black-eyed beans, 9
Black gram, 9
    black gram in a spicy cream sauce, 61
Black-eyed beans and potato curry, 62
Bombay duck pickle, 48
Bombay potato, 66
*Bomil achar*, 48
Bottle gourd, 9
    bengal gram and bottle gourd curry, 62
    rice layered with lentils and gourd curry, 26
Bread
    leavened bread, 22
    roasted unleavened bread, 22
    unleavened bread roasted with ghee, 21
*Bumbai aloo*, 66
*Butta salan*, 72
Buttermilk, 90

Casserole
    hot sweet and sour duck casserole, 47
Cauliflower
    curried cauliflower, 66
*Chai sherbet*, 90
*Chappati*, 22
*Chawal*, 24
Cheese, 9
    curried mushrooms, peas and Indian cheese, 71

Chicken
    chicken curry, 41
    chicken in a red hot sauce, 45
    chicken in spicy onions, 46
    chicken mulligatawny, 14
    fragrant rice with meat, 24
    Moghul style chicken, 44
    rice layered with chicken and potatoes, 18
    stuffed roast chicken, 40
    Tandoori chicken, 38
Chickpeas, 9
    curried chickpeas with potato cakes, 60
Chilli
    green chilli pickle, 76
    green chillis, 9
    hot chilli and garlic dipping sauce, 80
    potatoes in a hot red sauce, 74
    powder, 8
    red chillis, 9
    South Indian pepper water, 14
Chipsticks, eggs cooked on, 42

Chutney
    mango chutney, 79
    tomato chutney, 79
Cinnamon bark, 8
Cloves, 8
Coconut milk, obtaining, 92
Coriander
    fresh coriander relish, 79
    leaves, 9
    powder, 8
    seeds, 8
Courgettes
    dry moong dhal with courgettes, 64
Cucumber
    cucumber sambal, 82
    cucumber curry, 74
Cumin
    black, 8
    powder, 8
    seeds, 8
Curry
    bengal gram and bottle gourd curry, 62
    black-eyed beans and potato curry, 62
    boiled egg curry, 42
    chicken curry, 41
    corn on the cob curry, 72
    cucumber curry, 74

    curried cauliflower, 66
    curried chickpeas with potato cakes, 60
    curried mince, 34
    curried mushrooms, peas and Indian cheese, 71
    curried spinach and potato, 70
    curried stuffed bell peppers, 73
    hot and sour meat and lentil curry, 56
    hot dry meat curry, 30
    leaves, 9
    Madras, 36
    mixed vegetable curry, 69
    Parsi prawn curry, 55
    rice layered with lentils and gourd curry, 26

*Dekchi badak*, 47
*Dhal chawal palida*, 26
*Dhal sherva*, 12
*Dhansak*, 56
*Doodhi channa*, 62
Drinks
    buttermilk, 90
    tea and fruit punch, 90
Duck
    hot sweet and sour duck casserole, 47

Eggs
    boiled egg curry, 42
    eggs baked on chipsticks, 42
    spicy omelette, 16
Exotic fruit salad, 81

Fennel seeds, 8
Fenugreek powder, 8
Fish
    Bombay duck pickle, 48
    fish kebabs, 48
    fried whole fish, 52
    pickled fish steaks, 51
    prawns and fish in herb sauce, 50
    stuffed fish, 54
Five-spice powder, 8
Fragrant rice with meat, 24
Fresh coriander relish, 79
Fritters, onion, 10
Fruit
    exotic fruit salad, 83
    Indian fruit salad, 82
    yoghurt salad, 78

Garam masala, 8
Garbanzo beans, 9
    curried garbanzo beans with potato cakes, 60
Garlic
    hot chilli and garlic dipping sauce, 80
Gentleman's toes, 9
Ginger, 9
Green cardamom, 8

Green chillis, 9
Green gram
    flavoured green gram and rice, 64
*Gucci mattar paneer*, 71
Gypsy beans, 9

*Hara dhaniya chutney*, 79
*Haré masalé me jingha aur macchi*, 50
Herbs
    prawns and fish in herb sauce, 50
*Hoa qua tron*, 81
Hot and sour meat and lentil curry, 56
Hot chilli and garlic dipping sauce, 80
Hot dry meat curry, 30
Hot lime pickle, 76
Hot sweet and sour duck casserole, 47
Hot tomato sambal, 80

Indian cheese, 9
Indian cooking
    equipment and utensils, 8
    ingredients, 9
    principles of, 8, 9
    spices, 8, 9
Indian ice cream, 88
Ingredients, 9

*Jingha aur bhendi*, 52
*Jingha gucci biryani*, 20

*Kachoomber*, 79
*Kakri ka salan*, 74
*Kalmino patio*, 55
*Karhi*, 10
*Kairi ki chutni*, 79
*Kashmiri murgh*, 45
Kashmiri-style lamb, 30
Kebabs
    fish cakes, 48
    mince kebabs, 34
    spicy kebabs, 32
*Kheema*, 34
*Kheer*, 84
*Kitchdee*, 64
*Kofta*, 32
*Korma*, 36
*Kozhi mulla-ga-tani*, 14
*Kulfi*, 88

*Lagan ki seekh*, 32
*Lal batata*, 74
Lamb
    curried mince, 34
    fragrant rice with meat, 24
    hot and sour meat and lentil curry, 56
    hot dry meat curry, 30
    Kashmiri-style lamb, 30
    lamb in a creamy sauce, 36
    mince kebabs, 34
    Moghul-style roast lamb, 28
    potato cakes with stuffing, 13

spicy kebabs, 32
Leavened bread, 22
Lemon, 9
Lentils
    hot and sour meat and lentil curry, 56
    lentil soup, 12
    lentils seasoned with fried spices, 58
    mince kebabs, 34
    rice layered with lentils and gourd curry, 26
    South Indian lentils and vegetables, 58
Limes
    hot lime pickle, 76
*Lohia aloo*, 62

*Macchi achar*, 51
*Macchli kebabs*, 48
Mace, 9
Madras, 36
*Madras attu erachi*, 36
*Makhan chaat*, 82
Mangoes, 9
    mango chutney, 79
    mango sorbet with sauce, 89
*Masala urad*, 61
*Mava raitha*, 78
Meat loaf, spicy, 32

Melon, 9
Mint, 9
*Mirchi ka achar*, 76
Mixed vegetable curry, 69
*Moghlai murgh*, 44
Moghul-style chicken, 44
Moong dhal
    dry moong dhal with courgettes, 64
*Murgh biryani*, 18
*Murgh do piyaza*, 46
*Murgh ka salan*, 41
*Murgh mussallam*, 40
Mushrooms
    curried mushrooms, peas and Indian cheese, 71
    rice layered with prawns and mushrooms, 20
Mustard seeds, 9

*Naan*, 22
Nigella, 9
*Nimbu achar*, 76
Nutmeg, 9
Nuts
    almond curd junket, 87
    almond flakes, 9
    pistachios, 9
    walnuts, 9

yoghurt salad, 78

Okra, 9
    prawns cooked with okra, 52
    stuffed okra, 68
Onions
    chicken in spicy onions, 46
    onion fritters, 10
    red onion, 9
    seeds, 9
Oranges, 9

*Palak aloo sag*, 70
*Paratha*, 21
Parsi prawn curry, 55
Pastry triangles with savoury filling, 16
Peas
    curried mushrooms, peas and Indian cheese, 71
Peppercorns, 9
Peppers
    curried stuffed bell peppers, 73
*Petis*, 13
*Phul chaat*, 82
*Phul gobi salan*, 66
Pickled fish steaks, 51
Pickles and relishes
    Bombay duck pickle, 48
    fresh coriander relish, 79
    green chilli pickle, 76
    hot chilli and garlic dipping sauce, 80
    hot lime pickle, 76
    hot tomato sambal, 80
Pistachios, 9
Pork
    hot dry meat curry, 30
    Portuguese pork, 34
*Poro*, 16
Portuguese pork, 34
Potatoes
    black-eyed beans and potato curry, 62
    Bombay potato, 66
    curried chickpeas with potato cakes, 60
    curried spinach and potato, 70
    potato cakes with stuffing, 13
    potatoes in a hot red sauce, 74
    rice layered with chicken and potatoes, 18
Prawns
    Parsi prawn curry, 55
    prawns and fish in herb sauce, 50
    prawns cooked with okra, 52
    rice layered with prawns and mushrooms, 20
Purple beans, 9

*Ragda petis*, 60
Red chillis, 9
Red gram, 9
Red mullet
    fried whole fish, 52
Red onion, 9
Rice
    Basmati rice, 9
    flavoured green gram and rice, 64
    fragrant rice with meat, 24

INDEX

plain boiled rice, 24
rice layered with chicken and potatoes, 18
rice layered with lentils and gourd curry, 26
rice layered with prawns and mushrooms, 20
rice pudding, 84
Roasted unleavened bread, 22
*Rogan josh*, 30
Round red chillies, 9

*Sabzi salan*, 69
Saffron, 9
*Sag gosht*, 35
Salads
avocado salad, 82
Indian fruit salad, 82
tomato salad, 78
yoghurt salad, 78
*Sali pur eeda*, 42
*Sambal kecap*, 80
*Sambal selamat*, 80
*Sambal tomat*, 80
*Sambhar*, 58
*Samosas*, 16
*Santra*, 9
*Shahi raan*, 28
*Shammi kebab*, 34
*Shirkhuma*, 84
*Sookha gosht*, 30
*Sookhi moong aur chingri*, 64

*Soovar vindaloo*, 34
Soup
chicken mulligatawny, 14
lentil soup, 12
South Indian pepper water, 14
yoghurt soup, 10
South Indian lentils and vegetables, 58
South Indian pepper water, 14
Spices, 8
Spicy kebabs, 32
Spicy meat loaf, 32
Spicy omelette, 16
Spinach, 9
curried spinach and potato, 70
steak and kidney with spinach, 35
Star anise, 9
Steak and kidney with spinach, 35
Sweetcorn
corn on the cob curry, 72

*Tali huvey macchi*, 52
Tamarind, 9
*Tamatar kasondi*, 78
*Tamatar rasam*, 14
Tandoori chicken, 38
*Tandoori murgh*, 38
*Tarka dahi*, 78
*Tarka dhal*, 58
Tea and fruit punch, 90

Tindla, 9
Toffee apples, 88
Tomatoes, 9
hot tomato sambal, 80
tomato chutney, 79
tomato salad, 78
Turmeric, 9

Unleavened bread roasted with ghee, 21

Vegetables
mixed vegetable curry, 69
South Indian lentils and vegetables, 58
Vermicelli, 9
vermicelli pudding, 84

Walnuts, 9

*Xing ren tou fou*, 87

*Yakhni pilau*, 24
Yoghurt
spiced yoghurt, 78
yoghurt salad, 78
yoghurt soup, 10